GOLD

B1+ Pre-First

NEW EDITION

Introduction to the Gold B1+ Pre-First Exam Maximiser

The **Gold B1+ Pre-First Exam Maximiser** is specially designed to help you improve your language skills and maximise your chances of success in the Cambridge English Qualifications: B2 First examination.

The **Exam Maximiser** will help you prepare for the exam by offering you:

- **further practice and revision** of all the important vocabulary, grammar and skills (reading, writing, listening and speaking) that you study in the **Gold B1+ Pre-First Coursebook**.
- guidance with the **strategies and techniques** you should use to tackle exam tasks.
- **exam-style exercises** so that you can practise using the strategies and techniques.
- a section on **useful language**.
- a complete **Practice test** which you can use for preparation. This means that you will know exactly what to expect in each paper and that there are no unpleasant surprises.

What is in each unit?

The **Exam Maximiser** follows the structure of the **Gold B1+ Pre-First Coursebook**. Each unit provides further work on the language, skills and exam strategies you looked at in the Coursebook unit.

There are **Vocabulary** sections which practise the words and expressions you studied in the Coursebook. You'll also learn some new words and expressions. Activities include exam-style tasks as well as more fun activities like crosswords and wordsearch grids.

Each unit has two **Grammar** sections which practise the same points you studied in the Coursebook. There are activities to practise and revise the grammar and to help you identify where you might see it in the exam.

The **Speaking** sections include activities to help you build your skills for the Speaking paper. There are activities on useful language and on strategies for making yourself understood, agreeing and disagreeing and so on. In these sections, you often listen to or read examples of candidates performing the speaking tasks and then complete the activities to develop your own speaking skills.

Every unit has a **Listening** section with an exam-style recording, so there is plenty of opportunity for you to practise your listening skills. As in the Coursebook, these tasks are based on the tasks you will see in the exam and are designed to help you begin your preparation. Often, there is a section helping you with vocabulary from the text that you might not have seen before.

Similarly, the **Reading** section in each unit gives you more practice in dealing with the kinds of tasks you have covered in the Coursebook. You will get some information about the exam and help with exam strategies and techniques. Like the Listening sections, many of the Reading sections have activities for you to practise unfamiliar words and phrases.

There is a **Writing** section in every unit, which will help you build skills you will need for the exam, as well as for everyday writing tasks. You will look at examples of other people's writing and learn how to improve your own. In some tasks you work on useful language or on planning and organising your writing, while in other tasks you write your own answers. You can check your written work against sample answers.

At the back of the book, there is a **Useful language** section, which includes language for important functions such as giving opinions, agreeing and disagreeing and making suggestions. There are also useful phrases for the Speaking and Writing papers.

Once you have worked through all the units, you will be ready to try the **Practice test** at the back of the book. If you do this under timed exam conditions, it will give you a good idea of what to expect in the exam itself and your results will help you understand what to focus on as you prepare for it.

How can I use the Gold B1+ Pre-First Exam Maximiser?

You can use it with your teacher or on your own. Most of the time, you will write your answers to the activities in the **Exam Maximiser** itself. Most of the questions have only one answer, so they are very easy to correct. If you have an **Exam Maximiser** with a key, you can do the activities at home and correct them yourself. If you have an **Exam Maximiser** without a key, you will probably do the activities in class or for homework and then your teacher will correct them or go through them with you in class.

You can use the **Exam Maximiser** to check that you have learnt the grammar and vocabulary in each unit of the Coursebook or to revise for tests and exams. The skills you will work on in the Reading, Writing, Listening and Speaking sections will help you improve your language skills in general, and prepare for the exam.

CONTENTS

Making contact

Listening
Multiple choice: short extracts
▶ CB page 7

1 ▶ 01 **You will hear people talking in four different situations. For questions 1–4, choose the best answer, A, B or C.**

1 You hear a man talking about a friend who lost her job. Why did his friend lose her job?
   A She spent too much time online.
   B She was not honest.
   C She was unwell.

2 You hear a girl talking about a time she used her mobile phone on public transport. Why was she upset?
   A She had lost her mobile phone.
   B Her mother phoned her unexpectedly.
   C Strangers listened to a private call.

3 You hear a boy talking about a postcard he sent to a friend. How did the boy feel about sending this postcard?
   A annoyed about the time it took to arrive
   B amused by his friend's reaction
   C embarrassed because it never reached his friend

4 You hear a woman talking about sending an email. What mistake did she make?
   A She accidentally deleted the email.
   B She sent the email to some people unintentionally.
   C She wrote some untrue things in the email.

Vocabulary
collocations: communication, family relationships
▶ CB page 7

1 **Choose the correct option in italics to complete the sentences.**

1 Let's *meet/get* together when you come to my city.

2 I've communicated with her by email a lot but we've never met face *by/to* face.

3 My friend and I often go online to *chat/discuss* about nothing in particular.

4 Only *near/close* relatives and very good friends were invited to the wedding.

5 I've *made/done* some good friends at uni – I hope we don't *miss/lose* touch.

6 My friend has just got *engaged/divorced* to her boyfriend.

7 I like to keep *in/on* touch with old school friends – especially those who have moved abroad.

8 I love having a big *extended/open* family – we're all very close and meet up quite often.

Grammar

present simple and present continuous
▶ CB page 8

1 Choose the correct option in italics to complete the sentences.

1 I *don't go/'m not going* to the school reunion next month.

2 Shh! I *try/'m trying* to work!

3 Tara *has/is having* a hard time trying to get the phone company to replace her mobile.

4 I *often misunderstand/'m often misunderstanding* what people mean in text messages.

5 Miguel *is/is being* a real whizz on the computer – he can do anything!

6 Jenny's flight *leaves/is leaving* at three o'clock. She's going to visit her cousin in Australia.

7 It *becomes/'s becoming* harder and harder to keep in touch with old friends.

8 I *visit/'m visiting* my cousin in hospital tonight.

2 Complete the email with the present simple or present continuous form of the verbs in brackets.

Hi Suzana,

I **(1)** .... (*really/look forward to*) the school reunion next week! **(2)** .... (*you/come*)? I hope so! I'm so happy that our old school **(3)** .... (*organise*) such an exciting event. I **(4)** .... (*remember*) so much about our school days. I can't wait to talk to everyone about what they **(5)** .... (*do*) these days. I **(6)** .... (*want*) to tell them about what I **(7)** .... (*study*) at college, too – it's so interesting!

The party **(8)** .... (*start*) at seven o'clock. Hope to see you there!

Love,
Zena

3 Look at the verbs in brackets in Activity 2. Do they describe states (S) or actions (A)?

4 Circle the state verbs in the box.

chat	communicate	depend	do	hear
like	lose	own	phone	smell

Use of English

Multiple-choice cloze
▶ CB page 9

About the exam:
In the exam, you read a text with eight gaps and choose from four possible answers for each gap.

Strategy:
• Read the whole text quickly so that you understand what it's about.
• Read each sentence containing a gap and think about what kind of word might fit in each gap (e.g. a noun, a verb, an adjective, a conjunction).
• Look at the words immediately before and after each gap to help you.
• Think about words that often go together (collocations), e.g. *catch a bus*, *keep in touch*.

1 Read the blog post and decide which answer (A, B, C or D) best fits each gap.

I love my new mobile phone

I just love my new mobile phone and I **(0)** *A spend* hours every day texting and chatting to friends online. I'm sure some people think I waste too much time playing around on it when I should be doing more useful things – **(1)** .... college work! Obviously, it's really helpful to talk to my friends about what we're doing on the course, but it's also so easy to go online to **(2)** .... things up.

My favourite app is a music one called My Tune. I've got all my music **(3)** .... on my phone, which means I can listen to my favourite **(4)** .... in bed – that often helps me to **(5)** .... asleep if I have things on my mind. I also love taking photos on my phone, which I then **(6)** .... with my friends on social media. I've become **(7)** .... as 'the Expert Photographer' in my group, though I don't really think I'm that good!

All in all, I really don't think that I could **(8)** .... without my phone!

0	**A** spend	**B** pass	**C** give	**D** have
1	**A** as though	**B** such as	**C** just as	**D** as if
2	**A** look	**B** read	**C** find	**D** check
3	**A** collected	**B** carried	**C** supplied	**D** stored
4	**A** streams	**B** chapters	**C** tracks	**D** units
5	**A** go	**B** get	**C** drop	**D** fall
6	**A** share	**B** divide	**C** split	**D** part
7	**A** known	**B** referred	**C** named	**D** called
8	**A** face	**B** manage	**C** remain	**D** stay

Reading
Multiple choice
▶ CB pages 10–11

About the exam:
In the exam, you read a text and answer six multiple-choice questions. Each question has four options to choose from. Only one option is correct.

Strategy:
- Read the whole text quickly so that you understand what it's about.
- Read each question and the four options very carefully.
- Scan the text quickly to find the information you need, and underline the part of the text where you think the answer is.
- Read the section more carefully in order to find which option is correct.
- Remember that the words in the question and the words in the text may be different. Make sure you identify words in the text which have a similar meaning to those in the question.
- Make sure you know why the other options are not correct (e.g. it may be true but the text doesn't say it; the text says the opposite; the text says it but it does not answer the question).

1 Look at the photo in the article. What is a holiday rep?

2 Read the title of the article. What kind of information do you think it will include?

3 Read the article quickly and answer the questions.

1 What sort of people is the job of holiday rep not suitable for?

....

2 How old do you need to be to have a job like this?

....

3 Which languages can be particularly useful for a holiday rep?

....

4 Where can you find advertisements for jobs as a holiday rep?

....

5 What do holiday companies give their reps free?

....

6 What hotel facilities are mentioned in the article?

....

4 Read the article again. For questions 1–4, choose the answer (A, B, C or D) which you think fits best according to the text.

1 According to Angela, which of the following qualities is the most important for a holiday rep?
 A the ability to be flexible
 B a confident personality
 C a sense of responsibility
 D the willingness to work long hours

2 In the second paragraph, Angela says that before she got the job, she
 A had travelled a lot in her free time.
 B knew quite a lot about geography.
 C spoke more than one language.
 D had taken an advanced qualification.

3 Angela says that in an interview you should
 A make yourself sound better than you are.
 B find out about the travel company online.
 C talk about the attraction of free travel.
 D be honest about what you know.

4 What does Angela like most about being a holiday rep?
 A earning a lot of money
 B going out with her colleagues
 C the smart clothes she gets to wear
 D getting free access to facilities

5 Choose the correct meaning (A or B) for the underlined phrasal verbs in the article.

1 believe in
 A be certain that something exists
 B be certain about an ability

2 deal with
 A take appropriate action in a situation
 B be concerned about a situation

3 send out
 A put in the post
 B advertise

4 stand out
 A be easy to see
 B be better than others

5 find out
 A discover
 B recover

6 get on (with)
 A continue doing
 B have a good relationship with

So you want to be a Holiday rep?
Read on!

My name's Angela and I'm a holiday rep. I love my job and it's the best way to make friends with people from all over the world. Holiday reps are responsible for making sure that the customer has a fantastic holiday. As a rep, you represent the holiday company you're working for, so above everything else, you have to be friendly, sociable and <u>believe in</u> yourself. You also have to be able to <u>deal with</u> all kinds of situations and if you're impatient or like regular working hours, then this isn't the job for you. In addition, you have to be ready to go anywhere in the world – you don't get to choose where you work. For example, one month you might be in the south of France and the next in South America!

You need to be at least eighteen to become a rep and although formal qualifications aren't necessary, getting a basic certificate in travel and tourism, like I did, will always be useful because there's a lot of competition for jobs. It's not as easy as you might think to get a job in the travel industry. It's helpful if you can speak other languages, especially French or Spanish. I only speak English, so I didn't really expect to get a job – but I did! It helps if you travel a lot yourself too. I didn't have much chance to do that before I became a rep, though I did have a good knowledge of where places are in the world.

There are a few ways you can find work as a holiday rep. Newspapers and travel magazines often advertise positions. And don't forget the internet, which is probably the most useful source of information! Travel companies <u>send out</u> application forms to people who are interested in working for them – read the form carefully and make sure your application <u>stands out</u>. If you do get an interview, remember you must answer questions truthfully – you'll quickly get <u>found out</u> if you pretend you can speak Greek or are familiar with a country you've never even heard of! One thing you should avoid is saying you want the job to get free holidays! It sounds silly, but you'd be surprised by how many people actually say that.

There are lots of cool things about being a holiday rep. The pay isn't the best in the world but in my opinion, the benefits of the job are worth far more than the pay packet. You get to see some amazing places and the people are fantastic – I keep in touch with a lot of the customers I look after. The nightlife with the other reps and customers can be fun too, if you <u>get on</u> with them! You get free accommodation as a rep. Don't be too excited about this – I'm staying in a tent in my current job, which isn't the most comfortable place to stay! You also get a uniform but the greatest thing of all for me is that you get to use everything at the resort you're working at – brilliant if there's a swimming pool or tennis courts because you don't have to pay to use them.

Grammar

verb patterns: -ing and infinitive
▶ CB page 12

1 Complete the email with the correct form of the verbs in the box.

do	eat	fish	go	see (x2)
spend	swim			

Hi Elisa,

I'm here on holiday in Hungary with my family. My grandparents are Hungarian, so it's great to be with people who know the country really well. We're staying in a cottage in the countryside and there's a lake nearby where we enjoy **(1)** .... every morning. I'd love **(2)** .... this at home too, but there's nowhere fun to go.

I'm also learning **(3)** ....! I'm not usually keen on fishing but my granddad makes it great fun. **(4)** .... all day in the sun is pretty tiring, so before we have dinner we take a short nap. I love **(5)** .... outdoors – the food definitely tastes better!

I'm looking forward to **(6)** .... you. Let's **(7)** .... that new action film when I get back. I'd better **(8)** .... now – my dinner's getting cold!

See you soon,
Pete

2 Find and correct the mistakes with infinitives in the sentences.

1 We'd better not to be late home – I have a lot of homework to do tonight.

2 I'd love go to Kenya on holiday. I've never been to Africa.

3 I can't wait get my new phone – it's got some fantastic apps!

4 Let's to buy a present for Mike's birthday. What do you think he would like?

5 Stephanie's hoping pass her travel and tourism exam. She worked really hard.

6 Joe's learning be a tour guide. He wants to work in Spain.

7 I've arranged have a new website built for my work.

8 You should to check your passport is valid before you travel.

Speaking

Interview: giving personal information
▶ CB page 13

About the exam:
In the exam, the examiner asks you some general questions about yourself, such as where you live, your hobbies, plans or experiences.

Strategy:
• Try to give an answer that is not too short but is also not long and complicated.
• Do not memorise answers because you will sound unnatural. Learn key words and give natural answers.
• Try to make a good impression by smiling and appearing confident.

1 Match the questions (1–10) to the answers (A–H). There are two extra questions.

1 Where are you from?

2 What do you like about living there?

3 Do you watch much television? Why/Why not?

4 How do you like to keep fit?

5 What did you do on your last birthday?

6 What is your main ambition? Why?

7 Are you very interested in fashion?

8 Tell us something about your best friend.

9 Where do you like to spend your holidays? Why?

10 Do you have a favourite hobby? What is it?

A It's very peaceful and the people are very friendly. Everyone knows each other. It's really pretty too.

B France. My home is in Beaulieu, a small village just outside Bordeaux. It's close to a lovely forest.

C I think I'd like to be a teacher of primary school children. I'd like to teach them English.

D Not a lot. I prefer to spend my time with my friends, playing games and chatting.

E I prefer to go somewhere nice and hot where I can relax – like Spain or Italy.

F I do a lot of painting and drawing – especially cartoons. I draw cartoons of famous people and give them to my friends. It's fun!

G I'm not very worried about what I wear. I like trendy things but I don't spend a lot of time thinking about clothes.

H I went to a big hotel with my family and we had a lovely meal there. It was good.

Writing
Essay ▶ CB page 14

About the exam:
In Part 1, you have to write an essay. There will be a question for you to answer and two notes giving ideas that you must include in your essay. You will also need to add one more idea of your own.

Strategy:
Make sure you write about both of the points in the notes and think of a third one of your own. You must give reasons and/or examples to support your opinions.

1 **Read the exam task and complete the essay below with the words in the box.**

| because | for | however | matter | mean |
| reason | so | think | | |

In your English class you have been talking about what makes a good friend. Now your teacher has asked you to write an essay.

> Are old friends always the best friends?
>
> **Notes**
> Write about
> 1 shared experiences
> 2 different personalities
> 3 .... (your own idea)

Write an essay using **all** the notes and giving reasons for your point of view. Write **140–190** words.

As we get older, our lives change. We meet different people and make new friends all the time, (1) .... our social network includes people who have been important at different times in our lives. But are the oldest friends really the best?

I (2) .... this is true for some people. The (3) ....
I say this is because these friends know you better than anyone else. They have shared important experiences with you and sometimes they know you better than you know yourself. (4) .... of that, they can give you really good advice even if you and your friends are very different kinds of people, with different personalities.

(5) ...., this is not always the case. Someone may have known you very well in the past but that does not (6) .... they still know you well now. Perhaps you have both changed. This is especially true if you have been out of touch for a while.

(7) .... me, the best friends are the ones you can rely on to give you support and to tell you the truth. It doesn't (8) ....
whether you've known them for ten months or ten years.

2 **Underline the parts of the essay where the writer covers the two points given in the notes. What is the third point – the writer's own idea?**

3 **Match the phrases (1–6) to their functions (A–F).**

1 Many people feel that …
2 That is why …
3 I strongly believe that …
4 Alternatively, …
5 In addition to this, …
6 For instance, …

A introducing a different point
B giving an example
C adding to something you've said
D giving a general point of view
E giving a reason
F giving your opinion

4 **Read the exam task and think of a point of your own to include. Make notes to plan your answer. Then write your answer.**

In your English class you have been talking about the best people to ask for advice. Now your teacher has asked you to write an essay.

> Is it better to ask family or friends for advice?
>
> **Notes**
> Write about
> 1 type of problem
> 2 relationships
> 3 .... (your own idea)

Write an essay using **all** the notes and giving reasons for your point of view. Write **140–190** words.

2 Changes

Vocabulary
describing feelings
▶ CB pages 16–17

1 Choose the correct option in italics to complete the sentences.

1 I was *surprised/surprising* when Eddy gave me a present because he never usually remembers my birthday.

2 The instructions were really *confused/confusing* – we didn't know what to do.

3 I lent my umbrella to Eva and she lost it. I was very *annoyed/annoying*.

4 We worked until midnight on the project. It was *exhausted/exhausting*.

5 Fred wore a tiger suit to the fancy dress party. It was very *amused/amusing*.

6 I spilt coffee all over Greta's new dress. She was very *upset/upsetting*.

2 Complete the sentences with the correct form of the words in brackets.

1 I love the history of fashion! I think it's .... (fascinate) to see how clothes have changed over the years.

2 Jenny always gets .... (worry) before acting in a play. She thinks she'll forget her lines.

3 If someone says I look good, I get .... (embarrass) and go red!

4 I can't watch horror films – I get .... (scare) when I go to bed!

5 Pete was .... (thrill) when he won £1,000 in the competition.

6 It was a rather .... (depress) book, but it was a good read.

3 Which two adjectives from Activity 2 are positive?

Speaking
Long turn
▶ CB page 17

About the exam:
In Part 2, you talk on your own for about a minute. You have to compare two photographs and then answer a question about them.

Strategy:
• Don't describe each photograph in detail. Compare them and then answer the question.
• The question will be printed above your photographs, so you can look at it to help you remember what to talk about.

1 ▶ 02 Listen and complete the examiner's instructions.

Your photos show people who are **(1)** .... in different situations. I'd like you to compare the photos and **(2)** .... the people have decided to wear special clothes in these situations.

2 ▶ 03 Look at the photos and choose the correct option in italics to complete a student's answer. Then listen and check.

(1) *Both/Either* pictures show people who are wearing special clothes, but they're in different situations. **(2)** *On/In* the first picture the skier is spending her free time enjoying herself, **(3)** *whereas/ although* in the second one the people are obviously working in a kitchen. This means they have different reasons for the clothes they've decided to wear. I think the skier is a girl. She **(4)** *needs/ must* to have clothes that will protect her against the cold weather on the mountain, **(5)** *so/because* she is wearing thick clothes. She **(6)** *probably/likely* chose them herself because she wants to look good when she's skiing. She's also wearing a helmet, **(7)** *in case/ so that* she falls and hurts herself.

The people in the second picture, **(8)** *however/whereas*, probably didn't choose their clothes themselves – they have to wear them because their clothes are important **(9)** *as/for* the job they're doing. I think they're baking a cake and they have to cover their hair and their ordinary clothes **(10)** *so that/because* the food they're cooking stays safe and clean. The clothes are **(11)** *too/also* special for chefs so that other people can identify them. They all look very **(12)** *interested/interesting* in their work.

Listening
Sentence completion
▶ CB page 18

About the exam:
In the exam, you listen to a monologue and fill in the missing words in ten sentences. The sentences will be in the same order as the information in the recording.

Strategy:
• Read the title. This gives you information about what you will hear.
• Read the sentences first and think about the type of information that might go in each gap.

1 You will hear a woman called Suzy Bower talking about winning the lottery. Read the sentences and match the gaps (1–6) to the types of information in the box. You will need to use some words more than once.

a country   a feeling   an object   a place

A lucky lottery winner

Suzy bought her first lottery ticket at the local **(1)** ...., and she won a lot of money.

Suzy felt **(2)** .... when she won because she wasn't sure how to spend the money.

The first thing Suzy bought for herself after winning was a **(3)** ....

Paying for a new school **(4)** .... pleased Suzy the most.

Buying a **(5)** .... helped a member of Suzy's family in their work.

Suzy's first trip to a foreign country was to **(6)** ....

2 ▶ 04 Listen and complete the sentences in Activity 1 with a word or short phrase. Then check your answers to Activity 1.

Vocabulary

dependent prepositions
▶ CB pages 18–19

1 Choose the correct option (A, B or C) to complete the sentences.

1 Which company do you work ....?
  A of   **B** by   **C** for

2 Don't make jokes .... Paul's new hairstyle!
  A about   **B** across   **C** on

3 I'm in trouble – I completely forgot .... Ellie's birthday!
  A to   **B** with   **C** about

4 I'm often asked whether winning the lottery has made a big difference .... my lifestyle.
  A with   **B** to   **C** around

5 The children laughed .... the dog wearing a funny hat!
  A over   **B** at   **C** up

6 I'm really proud .... my younger sister.
  A about   **B** with   **C** of

7 This song always reminds me .... my dad – it's his favourite.
  A of   **B** over   **C** around

8 I love spending money .... presents for my friends.
  A for   **B** by   **C** on

Grammar

present perfect and past simple
▶ CB page 19

1 Choose the correct option in italics to complete the sentences.

1 *Have you ever bought/Did you ever buy* a lottery ticket?

2 *We've watched/watched* an interesting documentary on dinosaurs last night.

3 *Have you thought/Did you think* about who you want to invite to the party yet?

4 *I've never won/never won* a tennis match because I'm so bad at it!

5 My brother*'s been/was* scared of cats since one *has scratched/scratched* him last year.

6 Kim*'s been/went* to South America – she*'s been/went* to Bolivia in 2017.

7 *I've been/was* so tired yesterday that I*'ve turned down/turned down* a trip to the theatre.

8 Gareth's *just got/just got* a new job working for an advertising company.

2 Find and correct the mistakes in the sentences.

1 I've been to London on a business trip last week.

2 Life changed over the last few years for animals that live in the polar regions.

3 I've worn cool clothes when I was a teenager.

4 Megan has got up early this morning and did her homework before lunch.

5 The town I live in grew a lot since we moved here.

6 Lately people became more conscious of the need for responsible tourism.

Reading

Gapped text
▶ CB pages 20–21

About the exam:
In the exam, you read a text with six missing sentences and choose the correct sentences from a list to fill the gaps. There will be one extra sentence which you do not need to use.

Strategy:
Look carefully at the sentences before and after the gaps, and use reference words such as *it, he, this, there,* etc. to help you choose.

1 Look at the photo and read the title of the text. What do you think you are going to read?

A an advertisement for a holiday

B a magazine article

C a review on a holiday website

2 Read the text again. Choose from the sentences (A–G) the one which fits each gap (1–6). There is one extra sentence which you do not need to use.

A My friends used to laugh that I had never taken a risk in my whole life.

B Hearing her talk about the place, the local people, the food and the weather persuaded me.

C After only a few days I did just that and made a big discovery about myself.

D This means that there's little opportunity to just sit back, chill out and 'smell the flowers' – as my grandmother used to say.

E In spite of this, I enjoyed myself far more than I thought possible.

F However, I certainly wasn't expecting the step back in time that I was about to take.

G Then the sensible side of my brain started to work.

Can a *HOLIDAY* completely change your life?

Most of us today lead increasingly stressful lifestyles. The time that we aren't actually at work or college is often spent <u>commuting</u> or doing more work at home. We've adapted to lifestyles in which every moment is planned for. [1]   So, holidays, however long or short, are <u>precious</u>. They give us time to <u>destress</u> and recharge our batteries for the rest of the year. However, as well as this, they can sometimes have another, long-term effect. It's something I know from first-hand experience.

Last year I rented a house in Italy from a colleague. She'd bought the place very cheaply and had it renovated over a couple of years. It was in an old hilltop town in the south and the photos of the view from her kitchen window were quite amazing. [2]   It would be a perfect holiday. What I wasn't prepared for was quite how <u>drastically</u> this break would affect my life.

I had been warned about the isolation of the town, two hours' drive in a rental car from the nearest airport. [3]   Streets, too narrow for cars, circled round and round the hilltop. Steep steps linked each level and were really hard on the leg muscles! I fell in love with the place immediately. I loved that there were no hotels, no tourists and that in a fortnight I met only one person who spoke very little English. I loved the friendliness of the people who smiled and spoke to me in fast Italian, not caring that I could <u>barely</u> understand them. And what I really loved was the quietness, and sitting at the kitchen table gazing at a view that was <u>to-die-for</u>.

They say that holidays give you the chance to <u>reassess</u> your life and make decisions about your future. [4]   I was happier than I'd ever been and it wasn't only the temperature or the view. It was the way of life. I'd had enough of deadlines and rushing through the day, barely stopping for breath. The noisy, polluted streets seemed as far from this place as the moon. I wanted to stay.

[5]   It came up with question after question. Where would I live? How would I earn any money? Could I bear losing all the facilities and services of a big town, and being so far away from family and friends? And the biggest one of all was, did I really have the courage it took to go from a comfortably secure life to something completely unknown? The questions chased each other round in my head all week.

[6]   This was true. But I surprised myself and everyone else: in the end, I listened to my heart and not my head and checked out houses for sale. I used my savings to buy a small house and now I live in my Italian town full time. I've started a small English school for local people and I also teach English online, so I'm not broke. Am I happy? <u>Ecstatic</u>. Do I ever regret the decision? Never! My advice? Choose your holidays carefully – you never know what they might lead to!

---

3 **Match the underlined words in the article to their meanings (1–8).**

1 relax after a worrying or busy time ....

2 extremely and suddenly ....

3 think about again ....

4 very valuable ....

5 almost not; only with great difficulty ....

6 extremely happy ....

7 travelling to work ....

8 excellent ....

Grammar
past simple, *used to* and *would*
▶ CB page 22

1 Choose the correct option in italics to complete the sentences. Sometimes both options are possible.

1 When I was a child, I *used to/would* have blond hair but now it's dark brown.

2 Tina *sent/would send* Angelo a text to arrange a time to meet last night.

3 Paolo *used to live/lived* in Rome when he was in college.

4 Every Sunday we *used to/would* sit by the fire and listen to my grandma telling stories.

5 Michaela *said/used to say* she enjoyed the party last Saturday.

6 On Saturday Grace and Joe *had/used to have* a meal in a restaurant and then saw a film.

2 Complete the blog post with the correct form of *used to* or *would*. Sometimes both are possible.

Life dreams

What did you want to be when you were a kid? I **(1)** .... dream of being a professional footballer. Even when I was really young, I **(2)** .... spend hours kicking a ball around in the street where I lived. I **(3)** .... have the best football or the smartest trainers but I had so much energy and passion for the sport. My mother **(4)** .... have to come and find me at mealtimes – I didn't hear her calling because I was so absorbed in my practice! I **(5)** .... watch every match on TV and I **(6)** .... know the names of all the footballers. Sometimes my uncle **(7)** .... take me to watch a live match and I loved it! I **(8)** .... have a really powerful kick but then I got injured and that was the end of my footballing dreams. I still watch my local team but I don't play anymore. I'm more into music these days and that's the focus of my ambitions now!

Use of English
Open cloze
▶ CB page 23

About the exam:
In the exam, you read a text and fill in eight missing words.

Strategy:
- Remember that the title gives you clues about the topic of the text.
- Before you start reading, think about what ideas might be mentioned in the text.
- Read the whole text first for meaning, and think about what type of word might go in each gap.

1 Look at the title of the article. What is the article about?

Does technology actually change our brains?

There **(0)** *are* many ways in which technology has changed our lives for the better. The internet means that we can communicate with anyone anywhere in **(1)** .... world, so people can keep up relationships more easily. Social media has changed the way we **(2)** .... friends. All the information we need can be found at the touch of **(3)** .... button.

All that seems great, **(4)** .... however positive the effects of technology are, there are also things we need to think **(5)** .... One question is whether playing computer games actually changes the way people concentrate: do we focus less effectively if we play them too much? And because **(6)** .... is so easy to find information through search engines, are we losing the ability to remember things **(7)** .... ourselves? Are our brains actually changing **(8)** .... of the way we use technology? And if so, are these changes good or bad?

2 Read the article in Activity 1 and think about what type of word goes in each gap. Match the gaps (1–8) to the words in the box.

article (x2)	linking word (x2)	preposition (x2)
pronoun	verb	

3 Complete the article in Activity 1 with the words in the box.

a	about	~~are~~	because	but	for
it	make	the			

Writing
Informal email/letter
▶ CB page 24

About the exam:
In Part 2, you choose one of three tasks to complete. One task may be to write a letter or email in response to part of a letter or email you have received. This may be informal or semi-formal.

Strategy:
Make sure you deal with all the points that are made in the email or letter extract.

1 Which of these phrases would you NOT find in an informal email or letter?

1 Many thanks for your email/letter of 8 June.
2 Thanks for your lovely email/letter.
3 I must also tell you about …
4 Would you kindly send me …
5 We had a really good time.
6 I look forward to your reply.
7 See you soon, …
8 Yours sincerely, …

2 Read the exam task and choose the correct option in italics to complete the email on the right.

> You have received an email from your Scottish friend Gemma. Read this part of the email and write your email to Gemma.
>
> > We've just moved into our new house and there's lots of work to do. At least we can choose how it looks, though. What would you do to make your dream house? It'd be great to have your ideas.
> >
> > Love,
> > Gemma
>
> Write your email in **140–190** words in an appropriate style.

> Hi Gemma,
>
> I thought I'd drop you a line to **(1)** *make/let* you know what I'd do in my perfect new house! You know that I love nature, so **(2)** *as/like* you can imagine, for me, the most important thing is the front garden. I'd like the first thing I see to be grass and flowers and things. When we moved here, I asked Tom and Fran to come round and we did the work on the garden together. It **(3)** *went/happened* really well.
>
> The next thing I'd do would be to paint all the rooms bright colours. I'd use a different colour for every room. Apart **(4)** *to/from* that, there would be candles everywhere. I **(5)** *extremely/absolutely* love them – I think they add warmth to a room.
>
> **(6)** *Anyway/Besides*, do write soon with your news and tell me how things are **(7)** *going/doing*. Something **(8)** *says/tells* me that you're going to be busy for months! I can come and stay and help you **(9)** *off/out* with any work you've got to do **(10)** *if/as* you like!
>
> Lots of love,
> Amy

3 Read the exam task and make notes to plan your answer. Then write your answer.

> You have received an email from your English friend Max. Read this part of the email and write your email to Max.
>
> > I've decided to completely change my bedroom. I want a new colour scheme and a new style of furniture. My parents are paying for it and they say I can do anything I like! You're really creative – any suggestions?
> >
> > Love,
> > Max
>
> Write your email in **140–190** words in an appropriate style.

3 Passions

Listening
Multiple matching
▶ CB pages 26–27

1 ▶ 05 You are going to hear four people talking about cookery courses they run at a college. Listen and match the speakers (1–4) to the courses (A–D).

A Only the best!   Speaker 1 ☐
B Eat well, stay well!   Speaker 2 ☐
C Fattening but fun!   Speaker 3 ☐
D Eat for less!   Speaker 4 ☐

2 Listen again and choose from the list (A–D) what each speaker says about their course.

A I hope to influence people's lifestyles.   Speaker 1 ☐
B My students are not satisfied with simple recipes.   Speaker 2 ☐
C I can't teach all the students who want to attend my class. Speaker 3 ☐
D I teach an unlikely combination of students.   Speaker 4 ☐

Vocabulary
collocations: pastimes
▶ CB page 27

1 Complete the second sentence so that it has a similar meaning to the first using the word given. Use between two and five words.

1 In the beginning it was difficult to hit the ball in a straight line, but I got better.
TOUGH
It .... first to hit the ball in a straight line, but I got better.

2 He's always had a fascination with motorbikes.
PASSIONATE
He's always .... motorbikes.

3 I nearly gave up learning German at school, but I didn't and now I speak it well.
STUCK
I nearly gave up learning German at school, but I .... and now I speak it well.

4 You can't become a top chef in only a few years.
LIFETIME
It .... to become a top chef.

5 I've been addicted to computer games since I was ten.
HOOKED
I .... computer games when I was ten.

2 Complete the article with prepositions.

Cup stacking championships

If you're interested **(1)** .... seeing young people who are passionate **(2)** .... their hobby and who are also amazingly good **(3)** .... it, don't miss the finals of the National Cup Stacking Competition at Swindon Arts Centre this Saturday afternoon. This is fast becoming a really popular activity and kids everywhere are mad **(4)** .... it. This Saturday, contestants from all over the country will show us their skill by putting cups on top of each other as quickly as they possibly can. You'll be fascinated **(5)** .... their speed! Think you'd be hopeless **(6)** .... it? Try it yourself after the competition, when some of the youngsters will hold a teaching session aimed at getting us all **(7)** .... cup stacking! Come along and check it **(8)** .... and who knows – maybe you'll get hooked **(9)** .... it too!

go, do and *play*
▶ CB page 27

3 Complete the sentences with the correct form of *go, do* or *play*.

1 Some of my friends .... voluntary work at the weekends.

2 My parents never .... clubbing when they were my age!

3 Do you fancy .... a board game this evening? I'm not going out.

4 I can't .... this crossword – it's way too difficult.

5 Eric and Lisa .... chess every Saturday afternoon.

6 I'd like to .... an evening class in car maintenance.

7 We're .... bowling tomorrow – why don't you join us?

8 My friend's sister is .... karate at school. She's really good.

Grammar
countable and uncountable nouns
▶ CB page 28

1 Read the article and look at the underlined nouns. Are they countable (C) or uncountable (U)?

——I love my job!——

I'm really lucky to work in a **(1)** job I love. I teach at a college which offers a fantastic range of evening classes for adults. I've always been passionate about **(2)** languages, especially my own – English. At the moment I'm working with a **(3)** group of adults who, for various reasons, missed out on schooling when they were younger and fell behind in their reading and writing **(4)** skills. I don't earn much **(5)** money but what I love about teaching this class is the students' desire to catch up. Also, they're really creative in their **(6)** work because they have life **(7)** experience. They're an interesting group of **(8)** people – they want to get as much **(9)** knowledge as possible and are keen to get the kind of **(10)** qualification they didn't get when they were younger. It's really inspiring and quite different from teaching **(11)** children. I hope I'll be able to do it for a very long **(12)** time!

2 Find and correct the mistakes in the sentences. Two sentences are correct.

1 Caroline has learned a great new recipe for a pasta and sauce in her Italian cooking class.

2 The good news are that Ellie has found a new job.

3 I'm really enjoying learning a Spanish in my evening class.

4 I'm hoping to get a teaching qualification in scuba diving – I love it so much.

5 It's important to get good advices from other people when you're choosing a career.

6 Where did you get all the informations for your project?

7 I wanted to buy my friend a bar of milk chocolate, but she preferred dark.

8 People often like to eat breads with soup.

9 We're expecting a rain this afternoon.

10 Evening classes are great way to learn new skills.

quantifiers ▶ CB page 28

3 Choose the correct option in italics to complete the sentences.

1 I'll give you *an/some* information about the fashion design course next time I see you.

2 Can you add milk to the shopping list? There isn't *much/many* left. We need *a few/a little* apples too. Oh, and we haven't got *some/many* oranges either – could you get *some/any* more while you're there?

3 There's only *a little/a few* coffee left – would you like tea instead?

4 Were there *much/many* people at the pool? There were *a lot/lots of* when I went the other day.

5 *Few/Little* children seem to enjoy playing outside these days. It's a pity.

6 Could I borrow *some/a little* of your maths books, please? I have to do *a few/a little* extra homework.

Speaking
Collaborative task ▶ CB page 29

About the exam:

In the exam, you and your partner discuss a question for two minutes. The examiner gives you some prompts to help you. There are five prompts. The examiner then asks you to make a decision.

Strategy:

• Interact with your partner. Remember: this is a discussion.
• Discuss each prompt fully before you move on to the next one.
• Don't worry if you don't have time to discuss all five prompts.
• Don't worry if you don't agree with your partner. Say what you think, and why.

1 Read the exam task and decide if the statements on the right are true (T) or false (F).

Here are some things young people often become very interested in. Talk together about why you think young people find these things interesting.

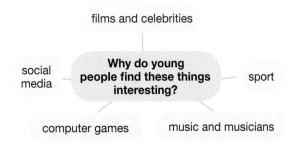

Why do young people find these things interesting?
- films and celebrities
- social media
- sport
- computer games
- music and musicians

1 You have to talk about everything young people are passionate about nowadays.

2 You have to say whether young people should take up these interests.

3 You have to identify what young people find interesting about the given points.

4 You have to take turns to give your own opinions.

5 You could talk about how the people feel when they do these things.

6 You have to talk about all the points given.

2 Match the students' comments (1–5) to the prompts in the exam task in Activity 1.

1 I think it's the fact that you can keep in touch with friends whenever you like that is so interesting – and it's easy to find out what everyone else is doing.

2 It's good for your health, but people often get obsessive about competition and winning.

3 Everyone has different tastes, so there's always something new that friends might tell you about, and that's interesting. It's great to increase the number of bands you listen to.

4 I think the private lives of actors are always interesting because they seem glamorous, and seeing them on screen is always great too.

5 I think it's really popular because it's so competitive, but it's also easy to access it at home. It's great fun to make friends and play against them.

3 Complete the useful phrases with the words in the box.

agree	as	downside	in	let's	on
point	think	what (x2)			

1 _____ begin with social media.

2 _____ you say, it's good for your health. It's also …

3 _____ my opinion, even if you're not good at it, you can always support a team.

4 Do you _____?

5 Let's move _____ to films and celebrities.

6 Don't you _____?

7 That's a good _____.

8 _____ do you think about this one?

9 The _____ is when winning becomes an obsession.

10 _____ you say about making friends is important. Also, …

4 Match the phrases in Activity 3 (1–10) to their functions (A–D).

A organising the discussion
B involving your partner
C giving an opinion
D referring and adding to your partner's comments

Reading
Multiple matching
▶ CB pages 30–31

1 Read the article about famous people who have done difficult things to raise money for charity. Which celebrity (A, B or C) raised the least money?

2 Read the article again. For questions 1–10, choose from the sections (A–C). The sections may be chosen more than once.

Which celebrity

had to use special clothing because of unexpected conditions? **1**

spent less time training than recommended? **2**

initially regretted accepting the challenge? **3**

passed an important date during the event? **4**

recovered from a health problem during the challenge? **5**

did something they had never tried before? **6**

needed to lose weight? **7**

failed to complete the challenge within the expected time? **8**

had previous experience of doing sporting challenges for charity? **9**

was welcomed by a large crowd at the end of the challenge? **10**

Celebrity challenges

★★★★★★★★★★★★★★★★★★★★★★★★★★

Every year celebrities push themselves to the limit – all because of a passion to help charities. Here are three of them.

A Eddie Izzard

Eddie Izzard is better known for his comedy and acting skills than his running! However, Eddie decided to set himself a big challenge to try to raise a lot of money for charity. He set out to run forty-three marathons across the UK. His aim was to run one marathon every day, six days a week, and he nearly did it! In fact, it took him slightly longer – fifty-one days. When he decided to go ahead with the marathons, he was heavier than he wanted to be and hadn't done a lot of running before. Some fitness experts worked out a nine-month programme for him to prepare, but Eddie only had five weeks! So, he trained hard and then set out on the challenge of a lifetime. And he succeeded. Despite blisters and sore toes, he ran and ran and returned home triumphant. He believes that it was his determination not to give up that saw him through the challenge, as well as the fear of letting down his charity. He ended up raising more than £200,000 online. Well done, Eddie!

B Alex Jones

Imagine spending two days and two nights climbing up a vertical rock face in the US. Then imagine you've had no experience of climbing before! This was the task that Alex Jones, a TV presenter, set herself a few years ago to raise money for charity. The Moonlight Buttress in Utah is a challenge for even experienced climbers, certainly not for a beginner. Luckily, Alex had the company of a climbing expert and a team to ensure her safety. She also received three months training before the climb. However, later Alex admitted to being in constant fear the whole time and was convinced that she had made a big mistake almost as soon as she'd started. When she finally reached the top, the first thing she did was to run over and hug the nearest tree! Alex, who turned thirty-seven during the climb, raised an amazing £650,000 for charity. What a way to spend your birthday, Alex!

C David Walliams

David Walliams is a popular TV comedy actor who has spent a lot of time in recent years doing swimming challenges for charity. He has raised large amounts of money by swimming across the English Channel and the Straits of Gibraltar, and in 2011 he swam 140 miles along the Thames River, finishing at Westminster Bridge in central London. David completed this marathon swim in eight days and it certainly wasn't an easy challenge. Because of the cold summer, the water temperature was low. When his skin started turning blue, he had to wear a wetsuit! Then, after a short time, he picked up a stomach illness – the Thames isn't the cleanest river! In spite of a fever and sickness, David continued. Luckily, he got better and completed his journey. Thousands and thousands of people cheered as he swam under the final bridge, and the final total donated to his online campaign was £1.1 million. What will it be next, David?

3 **Complete the sentences with the correct form of the underlined phrasal verbs in the article on page 21. Use the words in brackets to help you.**

1   When I was in Spain on holiday, I .... (*caught*) an illness and was in bed for a week.

2   I think I really .... (*disappointed*) my parents when I failed my exams last year.

3   We decided to .... (*continue*) with our plans to run ten miles for charity although the weather was terrible.

4   We got lost on our walk and .... (*found ourselves*) five kilometres away from home.

5   I .... (*planned*) to revise for three hours every day but I never did the full three!

6   I spent ages looking for our dog, which had run away. I nearly .... (*stopped*) but then I heard barking in the trees behind our house.

Grammar

present perfect simple and continuous
▶ CB page 32

1 **Choose the correct option in italics to complete the sentences.**

1   I've *counted up/been counting up* the money we raised for charity. I'll carry on after lunch.

2   Have you ever *tried/been trying* gardening? It's not as boring as people think.

3   My brother has *trained/been training* for the marathon for weeks.

4   I've *rung/been ringing* Maria all afternoon. I think she's at the gym.

2 **Complete the blog post with the past simple, present perfect simple or present perfect continuous form of the verb in brackets.**

Use of English
Word formation
▶ CB page 33

About the exam:
In the exam, you complete eight gaps in a text. You are given words in capitals at the end of some of the lines, to use in the correct form in the gaps.

Strategy:
• Read the title and the whole text first for meaning.
• Look at each gap and decide what type of word you need (e.g. a noun, a verb or an adjective).
• Look at the word in capitals and decide how to make it fit the gap.
• Remember: sometimes you may need to make two changes to a word.

1 **Make nouns from the words below using the suffixes in the box.**

-hood	-ian	-ing	-ion	-ment
-ness	-or/-er	-ship		

Example:
dance   ....*dancer*........ , ...*dancing*........

1   teach   ...., ...

2   library ....

3   invent ...., ...

4   replace ....

5   friend ....

6   sad   ....

7   child   ....

8   develop ...., ...

9   hesitate ....

My unusual hobby: clog dancing

I'm passionate about rhythm and I **(1)** .... (*always/be*) into dance forms that are percussive – in other words, where you make a noise on the floor with your feet! I **(2)** .... (*do*) tap dance classes since I was ten and more recently I **(3)** .... (*take up*) clog dancing – a traditional form of dance that, where I come from, **(4)** .... (*grow up*) in factories in the late 1800s. The story goes that factory workers, who **(5)** .... (*wear*) wooden shoes for work, started dancing in them and imitated the sounds that the factory machines made.

Clog dancing **(6)** .... (*probably/be*) around for hundreds of years although it was considered a minority interest. However, it **(7)** .... (*regain*) its popularity and there are festivals all over the country. My own dance group **(8)** .... (*just/raise*) over £1,000 for charity by doing a 'dance-a-thon', where we **(9)** .... (*dance*) non-stop for twelve hours! Since then, we **(10)** .... (*work*) really hard on a new dance routine and we're going to enter a national competition. We'll be on stage in front of hundreds of people. I know I'll be nervous. It'll be great fun, though.

2 Read the blog post. Use the word given in capitals at the end of some of the lines to form a noun that fits in the gap in the same line.

♪ Playing music: the hidden advantages

I've been playing the piano since I was five. It wasn't my choice originally – my mum made the **(0)** _decision_ for me. My friends thought **DECIDE**
it was a big **(1)** .... as I had three **COMMIT**
lessons every week, and actually I had the
same **(2)** .... – I hated it. This was **REACT**
because I had no **(3)** .... at all and **DEDICATE**
I just wanted to be doing fun stuff like everyone else.

After a while my teacher started entering me
for **(4)** .... – I think she hoped one day **COMPETE**
I might become a famous **(5)** .... The **MUSIC**
other participants seemed to have a sense
of **(6)** .... about taking part, but **EXCITE**
I never did. I absolutely hated them and
couldn't wait for them to be over. I just
couldn't see the point and, to my teacher's
(7) ...., I almost never won. **DISAPPOINT**

Now that's all changed. I've developed a
love for music, and it brings me joy. It's also
given me more confidence in life. I'm so glad
my mum gave me the **(8)** .... and **ENCOURAGE**
support that she did.

Music definitely has unexpected benefits!

Writing
Review
▶ CB page 34

About the exam:
In Part 2, one of the options may be a review (of a book, film, play, place, product, etc.).

Strategy:
- It doesn't matter if you like or dislike what you are reviewing, but give examples to support your opinion.
- Include general information, say why you liked/disliked it and make a recommendation.
- Use an informal style to engage the reader.

1 Read the exam task and choose the correct option in italics to complete the review below.

You recently saw this notice in an international student magazine.

Have you seen a good documentary recently? What was special about it? Send us your review and we'll post the three best ones on our website.

Write your review in **140–190** words in an appropriate style.

Man on Wire
★★★★☆

I enjoy documentaries and one **(1)** *of/from* the most interesting I've ever seen is the British-made *Man on Wire*, which **(2)** *came/made* out in 2008. It **(3)** *took/won* many awards at the time and is now considered a **(4)** *classical/classic*.

Man on Wire **(5)** *follows/plays* the true story of Robert Petit, a French tightrope walker. Robert developed his particular obsession with tightrope walking when he was ten years old, and he always wanted to walk in extremely high places. In 1974 his dream finally **(6)** *became/came* true. He walked across a wire stretched between the Twin Towers in New York, 1,350 feet up in the air, not just once **(7)** *although/but* eight times!

The first remarkable thing about this documentary is the way the director **(8)** *divides/combines* real film and photographs from 1974 with more recent interviews. The second is that the documentary is filmed like a crime film.

I found *Man on Wire* **(9)** *fascinated/fascinating*, funny and entertaining. It's amazing to see someone overcoming extreme challenges, however impossible it may have **(10)** *seemed/shown* at first!

2 Make notes to plan your own answer to the exam task in Activity 1. Then write your answer.

4 A sense of adventure

Reading
Multiple choice
▶ **CB pages 38–39**

1 Read the article quickly and choose the correct option in italics to complete the sentences.

1 The research boat was near *South America/South Korea/South Africa*.

2 The shark was *three/three and half/five* metres long.

3 The shark was *taken to a research centre/put back in the sea/killed*.

2 Read the article again. For questions 1–6, choose the answer (A, B, C or D) which you think fits best according to the text.

1 In the first paragraph, the writer suggests that many people
   A know a lot about marine biology.
   B enjoy reading about marine research projects.
   C often watch animals in their own gardens.
   D would like the same experiences as marine researchers.

2 The scientists were in the boat because they wanted to
   A catch some sharks.
   B observe the sharks' behaviour.
   C talk to the fishermen in the area.
   D check what food attracts sharks.

3 What were some of the crew members doing when the shark jumped onto the boat?
   A They were putting some food in the water.
   B They were splashing the water to make the sharks jump.
   C They were watching sharks swimming by the boat.
   D They were waiting quietly.

4 What did the shark do when it landed on the boat?
   A It fell on and hurt a crew member.
   B It broke some things on the boat.
   C It pushed part of its body out of the boat.
   D It prevented the men on the boat from moving.

5 After the first rescue, the shark had difficulty
   A getting free from the ropes.
   B using its tail to move.
   C swimming back to the open sea.
   D getting off the deck of the boat.

6 How does Gennari feel about the event?
   A sure that the shark did not intend to jump on the boat
   B worried that the shark might attack again
   C puzzled by the reason for the shark's jump
   D amazed that the shark could jump so high

Great white shark jumps onto research boat

Marine researchers lead an interesting and exciting life. They do important work and visit places all round the world that normal people can only dream of. They find and observe animals and plants that most of us only ever see on TV and in books. However, life became a little more exciting than expected for some scientists in the sea off the coast of South Africa a few years ago.

Several scientists were conducting a survey of the shark population when they suddenly got much closer to a shark than they wanted! The scientists were on board a research boat called *Cheetah* and they wanted to attract white sharks. These wonderful animals are known to jump out of the water when they see some prey. The scientists were keen to see this type of activity.

Dorien Schröder was the team leader at Oceans Research, the organisation conducting the survey. She said that after more than an hour of shark activity around the boat, the waters at the front of the boat had been quiet for five minutes. 'Next thing I know, I hear a loud splash and see a white shark jump out of the water directly over the men who were throwing sardines into the sea!'

Schröder pulled her colleague to safety before the shark, weighing about 500 kg, landed on top of the bait and fuel containers. It was about three metres long! At first, half of its body was outside the boat but in a panic, the shark pushed its way further on to *Cheetah*. It cut fuel lines and smashed equipment before becoming trapped between the containers and the back of the boat. The crew ran to the front of the boat for safety.

Schröder poured water over the shark to keep it alive and the crew tied a rope round its tail. A second boat then towed Cheetah to the port, with the shark still on deck. Eventually, the big fish was lifted off by machinery and then lowered back into the water.

Though the shark swam away, it was unable to find its way out of the harbour and soon ended up on the beach. With Oceans Research's co-director Enrico Gennari, an expert on great white sharks, the team tried many ways to rescue the animal. Finally, they used ropes to pull it through the harbour and back out to sea. The ropes were then removed and the animal swam away.

Gennari said it was the first time he had heard of a great white shark jumping onto a research boat. He guessed that the animal had jumped about three metres out of the water to be able to land on the boat. As for the cause of the shark's behaviour, Gennari said it was almost certainly an accident and not an attack on the boat. In the dark water, the big fish might have thought that the boat's shadow was prey. 'It's all speculation,' he said. 'But sometimes a shark jumps out of the water when it feels another shark underneath it. They move like a flying fish and end up several metres away.'

In this case, both scientists and shark had a narrow escape. But there can't be many scientists who have had the chance to get so close to a great white shark. And there can't be many sharks that have got so close to their observers!

---

3 Match the words from the article (1–6) to their meanings (A–F).

1	prey	A	unable to find a way out
2	bait	B	small animals that big animals hunt for food
3	trapped	C	people who work on a boat
4	crew	D	used a vehicle to pull something
5	rope	E	food used to attract animals
6	towed	F	thick line used to tie things

4 Complete the collocations in italics with words from the article.

1 I think writers .... very interesting *lives*.

2 We're going to .... *a survey* at school to find out who has had the most exciting holiday.

3 When the cruise liner was in port, we went .... *board* and had a look round. It was amazing!

4 We couldn't see the performers on stage, so we *pushed our* .... *to the front*.

5 We rescued a bird with a broken wing and helped .... *it alive* by giving it some bread before we took it to the vet.

6 Janine had a .... *escape* last week when her bike nearly went into a river!

Grammar
narrative tenses
▶ CB page 40

1 **Match 1–6 with A–F to make a story.**

1 It was a great day for snowboarding.
2 I had got all my gear ready the night before,
3 The slopes had just opened when
4 I was speeding down the mountain on my board when
5 I couldn't see what it was but
6 It was a huge white swan flying over the slopes!

A so I set off to the mountains nice and early.
B It flew over my head and into the distance. What a strange sight!
C I saw something in the air ahead of me.
D I arrived.
E it was coming towards me very quickly!
F The sun was shining and the snow was fresh.

2 **Complete the story with the past simple, past continuous or past perfect simple form of the verbs in brackets.**

time phrases
▶ CB page 40

3 **Cross out the option in italics which is NOT possible. You need to cross out two options in two sentences.**

1 *Afterwards/As soon as/When* I reached the hotel, I went for a swim in the pool.
2 *While/When/As soon as* Sue had booked the travel arrangements, she rang to tell me.
3 Ed cooked dinner for Jo *after/when/by the time* she got home from her trip.
4 *While/During/After* the sun was going down, we were having tea on the balcony.
5 I was really hungry *by the time/afterwards/when* I had finished skiing.
6 *During/While/When* Jay was collecting the luggage, he dropped a suitcase on his toe.
7 The flight was so tiring that *as soon as/by the time/when* I got home, I went to bed and slept for twelve hours.
8 *During/When/While* my trip to Morocco, I went to see the city of Casablanca.

A PARTY IN OPORTO

What a trip I had last month! My friend Noela **(1)** .... (*invite*) me to her twenty-first birthday in Oporto, Portugal. She studied English with me in London last summer and we had stayed in touch. This was a chance to see her again and I **(2)** .... (*look forward to*) it.
I **(3)** .... (*already/book*) my flights and accommodation, found a great outfit to wear and bought a cool gift for Noela.

On the day of the party, everything was going really well. I **(4)** .... (*arrive*) in Oporto the night before, the weather was beautiful and I was really excited to be in a city I **(5)** .... (*never/be*) to before. I set off from my hostel in the direction of the hotel where the party was taking place. I got onto the tram and **(6)** .... (*look*) at the map of the city in my guidebook when I had a sudden feeling that I **(7)** .... (*go*) in the wrong direction!

I quickly got off the tram and looked around. Then I **(8)** .... (*realise*) I was lost in a strange city

without knowing a word of Portuguese! Fortunately, a very kind girl saw me looking at my map and she asked me in English where I wanted to go.
I **(9)** .... (*explain*) the situation and then she smiled and pointed across the road.
I **(10)** .... (*stand*) opposite the hotel! I had been going in the right direction after all!

Speaking

Long turn
▶ CB page 41

1 ▶ 06 Listen to the examiner's question and look at the photos below. Then complete the sentences from a student's answer with the words in the box.

if	imagine	looks	might	probably	sure

1 The people in the first picture are _____ at an airport.

2 I _____ the people at the airport are feeling pretty fed up.

3 It looks as _____ the people in the second picture are trying to get on an underground train.

4 It _____ be during the rush hour.

5 One girl at least _____ tired.

6 I'm _____ it's really boring to wait for ages like that.

2 ▶ 07 Now listen to three follow-up questions (1–3). Match them to the answers (A–C).

A At a train station, because it's more crowded and usually there's more to do at an airport.

B It's OK, but I sometimes get a bit scared when we take off and land.

C Yes, I love it. It's quick and easy, and it's fun to watch all the people.

Listening

Sentence completion
▶ CB page 42

1 ▶ 08 You will hear a man called Jack talking about a trip he made to the Arctic. Listen and answer the questions.

1 What time of year did he go on his trip?

....

2 Did he enjoy the experience?

....

3 What does he want to do next time he visits the Arctic?

....

2 Listen again and complete the sentences

A winter trip to the Arctic

The fact that it was a **(1)** _____ trip with friends made it even more exciting for Jack.

Jack uses the word **(2)** _____ to describe what he expected his trip to be like.

Jack and his friends stayed in **(3)** _____ during their trip .

Jack was amazed that there was so much **(4)** _____ in the Arctic.

Jack felt pleased that he had packed lots of **(5)** _____ for his trip.

Jack describes some of the information he got from local husky trainers as **(6)** _____.

Jack was disappointed that he couldn't see any husky **(7)** _____ while he was there.

Jack says that the Northern Lights can be seen on **(8)** _____ and clear nights.

Jack compares the appearance of the Northern Lights to **(9)** _____.

Jack is planning to revisit the Arctic in **(10)** _____.

Vocabulary
extreme adjectives
▶ CB page 43

1 Find extreme adjectives in the wordsearch for the adjectives in the box.

bad	big	cold	hot	hungry		
interesting		loud	scary	small		tired

t	d	o	d	i	k	v	a	n	n	o	t
s	t	f	r	e	e	z	i	n	g	c	b
s	e	e	x	h	a	u	s	t	e	d	o
c	j	t	r	t	r	f	p	s	e	k	i
f	z	s	v	r	i	i	e	e	p	e	l
s	t	a	r	v	i	n	g	n	r	e	i
j	e	j	e	r	d	f	y	c	i	o	n
t	x	o	f	a	h	j	y	f	o	n	g
f	a	s	c	i	n	a	t	i	n	g	g
t	e	r	r	i	b	l	e	e	n	a	e
e	n	o	r	m	o	u	s	j	p	g	c

2 Complete the sentences with adjectives from the wordsearch in Activity 1.

1 When the tree crashed down in our garden, the noise was ....

2 I hadn't eaten all day and I was .... by the time I got to the hotel.

3 I have a scar on my hand because of the accident but you can hardly see it – it's so ....

4 The bus driver drove very dangerously and for me the whole journey was .... !

5 The temperatures dropped a lot overnight and in the morning it was ....

6 It was a lovely meal but it cost my parents an .... amount of money.

Grammar
subject/object questions
▶ CB page 44

1 Read the story and choose the correct option (A or B) in the questions below.

All's well that ends well

Jake and Sarah Mellor have just returned from what should have been a sunny, romantic getaway. Jake had planned to ask Sarah to marry him once they had arrived at a luxury hotel in the romantic Indian city of Udaipur. But Jake hadn't done his research properly and the couple arrived in the middle of the monsoon season! The weather was absolutely terrible! Poor Jake's plans of getting down on one knee outside one of the city's beautiful palaces suddenly didn't seem like such a good idea in the pouring rain.

But Jake wasn't a person to give in easily and he approached the manager of the hotel they were staying in to ask if the chef could prepare a special meal with a diamond engagement ring hidden inside it for his wife-to-be. Of course, the hotel manager was happy to help Jake and promised a fabulous dinner in the restaurant overlooking a nearby lake.

The meal arrived and Sarah was enjoying the delicious food when she suddenly bit on something hard. 'I thought I had broken a tooth!' she laughed. 'But when I saw the ring and Jake asked me to marry him, I said *yes* straightaway.' The couple plan to get married in a palace in Udaipur – in the dry season, of course!

1 **A** Where did Jake and Sarah go on holiday?
  B Where Jake and Sarah went on holiday?

2 **A** Where the couple did stay in the city?
  B Where did the couple stay in the city?

3 **A** What Jake planned to do?
  B What did Jake plan to do?

4 **A** Who did Jake ask to help him?
  B Who asked Jake to help him?

5 **A** Who cooked a special meal?
  B Who did cook a special meal?

6 **A** What Sarah did think she broke?
  B What did Sarah think she had broken?

2 Match the answers (A–F) to the questions in Activity 1 (1–6).

A	the hotel manager	D	in a luxury hotel
B	Udaipur	E	a tooth
C	ask Sarah to marry him	F	the hotel chef

Use of English
Key word transformation
▶ CB page 45

1 Complete the second sentence so that it has a similar meaning to the first sentence, using the word given. Do not change the word given. You must use between two and five words, including the word given.

1 I think it's going to rain.   **LOOKS**
   It .... it's going to rain.

2 My dad became a pilot ten years ago.   **FOR**
   My dad .... ten years.

3 I hurt my leg during the football match.   **WHILE**
   I hurt my leg .... football.

4 It was extremely cold last night.   **ABSOLUTELY**
   It .... last night.

5 Jo arrived late, so we missed the bus.   **UP**
   Jo .... , so we missed the bus.

6 In my opinion, he was right.   **ASK**
   If .... , he was right.

Writing
report
▶ CB page 46

1 Read the exam task. Which of the points below do you think should NOT be included in the report?

> You have recently been on an activity holiday with some friends. You have been asked to write a report for the company that organised the trip. In your report you should explain what activities you did on the trip, say what was good or bad about them and make recommendations for future trips. Write your **report** in **140–190** words in an appropriate style.

1 how you travelled
2 what the food was like
3 what activities you did
4 what was good or bad about the activities
5 recommendations for changes
6 what the weather was like

2 Read a student's answer and check your ideas.

Introduction
(1) The aim of this report is to outline and assess the activities on our recent activity holiday and make recommendations for future holidays.

Activities
There were many different types of activities to choose from, including climbing, rafting, swimming and football. I took part in the climbing.

Assessment of the activities
Although everything was well-organised, there was a lot of waiting around for people who arrived late. (2) This meant that we lost time and also caused frustration. However, the organisers of each activity were friendly and helpful, and made sure that we all had a good time even if we were beginners.

Recommendations
(3) It is vital that each activity should start on time even if some people are missing.
(4) There should be more equipment available to borrow as some of us had to buy our own climbing equipment, which was expensive.
(5) It would be nice to have more social activities in the evening, such as musical evenings as there was not much to do once it got dark.

Conclusion
(6) Overall, the activities were very enjoyable and if the recommendations are followed, the experience can be even better.

3 Match the underlined words/phrases in the report (1–6) to these words/phrases with a similar meaning (A–F).

A   It's important to …
B   As a result, …
C   We strongly recommend that there is…
D   The purpose …
E   On the whole, …
F   One suggestion would be …

4 Make notes to plan your own answer to the task in Activity 1. Then write your answer.

5 The consumer society

Vocabulary

shops and shopping
▶ CB pages 48–49

1 Read the clues and complete the puzzle. What's the hidden word? What does it mean?

1 People usually do this in shops when they don't particularly want to buy something.
2 The name of a product or a group of products made by a company.
3 People use this when they don't want to pay for something immediately.
4 A small image that represents a company.
5 You can buy and sell things here – it's usually outside.
6 This is one of a group of shops which are run by the same company (two words).
7 This type of shop sells things which are not new (two words).

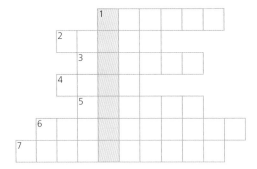

2 Complete the blog post with the correct form of words from Activity 1. You must use one of the words twice.

I must admit I'm a bit of a shopaholic. I love all sorts of shopping, whether it's in a shopping centre or an outside street **(1)** _____, and I especially like looking for **(2)** _____. Whenever there's a sale advertised, I'm there! Sometimes I just **(3)** _____ but other times I spend way too much. I try not to buy things on **(4)** _____, though, because I don't like being in debt and often if I haven't got much money, I check out the **(5)** _____ things in charity shops. You can often get good **(6)** _____ when you buy designer items there. Mind you, I'm not that worried about having a famous **(7)** _____ on everything I buy. But I do have a thing about designer bags. Gucci and Hermés are my favourite **(8)** _____, so I usually go for those.

Listening
Multiple matching
▶ CB page 49

1 ▶ 09 **Listen to four people talking about shopping for presents. Match the speakers (1–4) to the people they are buying a present for (A–E). There is one extra letter which you do not need to use.**

A   a friend   Speaker 1 ☐
B   a sibling   Speaker 2 ☐
C   a cousin   Speaker 3 ☐
D   an uncle   Speaker 4 ☐
E   him- or herself

2 **Listen again and choose from the list (A–E) what each speaker says about the experience. There is one extra letter which you do not need to use.**

A   The credit card didn't work.   Speaker 1 ☐
B   I had too little time.   Speaker 2 ☐
C   The shop was too crowded.   Speaker 3 ☐
D   The assistant was unhelpful.   Speaker 4 ☐
E   It was difficult to find something to buy.

Grammar
future forms
▶ CB page 50

1 **Find and cross out one extra word in six of the sentences.**

1   I'm going to meet my friend at the shopping mall on Saturday.

2   I think the shop will be close early today as it's a holiday tomorrow.

3   Do you think we will to get home by six tonight?

4   I'm going playing golf with Susie this afternoon.

5   I will to explain to my friend why I can't come to the party next week.

6   The bus leaves at 11.00, so I'm going to get to the bus station at 10.45.

7   I might to visit my uncle when I go to the city next week.

8   I will definitely be home by seven tonight, so we will be able to discuss the situation then.

9   Are you coming to the match this evening?

10   The film will starts at eight, so we'll have to be at the cinema by 7.30.

2 **Cross out the option that is NOT possible in each sentence.**

1   *I'm taking/I'm going to take/I take* that new phone back to the shop this morning – it isn't working properly.

2   *I'll meet/I'm meeting/I'm going to meet* Tina at the leather market at 3 p.m. She wants to buy a new bag.

3   Where do you think *I'm getting/I might get/ I'll get* the best deal on a second-hand car?

4   Oh no! The website's crashed on the payment page. *I'll have to/I'm having to/I'm going to have to* start again!

5   I think *I'll look/I look/I might look* at some of those price comparison websites for travel insurance later. It depends how tired I am after work.

6   The bank *might close/closes/will close* at 4 p.m. today – it says so on their website. So I'd better go and pay the money in now.

3 **Complete the email with the correct future form of the verbs in brackets. Sometimes more than one form is possible.**

Hi Charlie,

What **(1)** .... (*you/do*) tomorrow? I'm going shopping. It's my twin brother and sister's birthday on Sunday and I've got lots to buy, so I **(2)** .... (*go*) into town after my classes. I **(3)** .... (*buy*) my sister a voucher and for my brother, an alarm clock – he loves his gadgets! I know they **(4)** .... (*be*) really pleased with those.

After shopping, I **(5)** .... (*meet*) some friends and we **(6)** .... (*have*) dinner at our favourite pizza restaurant. One of my friends, Steph, hasn't been before but I'm sure she **(7)** .... (*like*) it. Then we **(8)** .... (*go*) to see a late-night film at the cinema, which **(9)** .... (*start*) at 11 p.m., but it depends how tired we are!

I **(10)** .... (*write*) again soon!

Love,
Elena

Speaking
Collaborative task
▶ CB page 51

1 Look at some sentences from a Part 3 discussion about shopping. Complete the phrases the students used to make and respond to suggestions with the words in the box. There are two extra words.

about	have to	let's	might	shall
sure	think	true		

1 OK, ... talk about how shops encourage people to spend money .

2 But don't you .... that might be difficult?

3 .... we talk about spending habits next?

4 It .... be better to try something less complicated though.

5 That might be ...., but people like buying new things.

6 I'm not too .... about that. There are lots of discounts these days.

2 Are the sentences in Activity 1 suggestions (S) or responses to suggestions (R)?

3 ▶ 10 Read the exam task and choose the correct words to complete the discussion on the right. Then listen and check.

> Some people think there is too much advertising on television nowadays, and other people disagree. Here are some things they think about. Talk to each other about whether there is too much advertising on television nowadays.

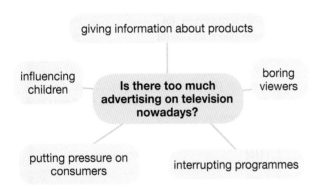

giving information about products

influencing children

boring viewers

Is there too much advertising on television nowadays?

putting pressure on consumers

interrupting programmes

A: So, let's think about advertisements influencing children. What do you think? Is advertising a bad thing for them?

B: **(1)** *Clearly/To be honest*, I don't think children really watch them – they probably ignore them. But if they do, I would say it's a bad thing to have a lot of advertisements on television, especially for sweets and sugary things.

A: I know what you **(2)** *say/mean*. Children can be easily influenced to want things that are bad for them, especially if the advert has music and cartoons to amuse them as well.

B: What about giving information about products? That's quite important for consumers.

A: You're **(3)** *OK/right*, but do you think advertisements always tell the whole truth?

B: It **(4)** *depends/can*. I suppose it's our responsibility to check out what they say.

A: That would be a problem **(5)** *while/if* we had to do it for all the advertisements on television! There seem to be advert breaks every ten minutes.

B: We **(6)** *might/could* be able to rely on most of them – after all, they are checked before they are broadcast.

A: True. But what annoys me is the way they interrupt a programme I'm really enjoying.

B: Yeah, I totally agree about that. There's nothing more annoying than having a dramatic moment spoiled by an advert.

A: So, **(7)** *could/maybe* people who record programmes and fast forward through the adverts are being clever!

B: Yes! But the **(8)** *problem/question* is, are there too many advertisements on television? I'd say there are.

A: I'm not too sure **(9)** *on/about* that. I think companies do need to advertise their products – that creates a good economy.

B: You have a point, though I don't think I **(10)** *can/might* agree with you.

Reading
Gapped text
▶ CB pages 52–53

1 Read the title of the article and choose the best definition for *swapped*.

A bought   B exchanged

2 Read the article. Choose from the sentences (A–G) the one which fits each gap (1–6). There is one extra sentence which you do not need to use.

A From the start, MacDonald insisted on meeting each person with whom he was dealing.

B I don't see it as any more strange than offering your time in return for a salary like most people in full-time jobs do.

C 'I was doing trades all over the place without spending any of my own money on petrol or plane fares,' he said.

D However, no one seems more surprised by his success than Kyle himself.

E This was even more remarkable as MacDonald had intended the whole thing to be 'just a bit of fun'.

F 'I only dealt with people I liked the sound of, or who seemed to genuinely support the idea of the website.'

G Why not see what people would give him in exchange for it?

3 Match the underlined words in the article to their meanings (1–6).

1 very strange ....
2 with no value ....
3 useful ....
4 looked quickly ....
5 very silly or unreasonable ....
6 not important ....

I swapped my paper clip for a house

Do you, like me, have a drawer somewhere at home full of different bits of rubbish which you think might come in <u>handy</u> some day? If so, the story of Canadian internet entrepreneur Kyle MacDonald may inspire you to take a closer look at what is hiding among the old pieces of paper and bits of string.

A few years ago, Kyle set out on what seemed a <u>ridiculous</u> and impossible project at the time – to trade a single paper clip for a house. He advertised this almost <u>worthless</u> item on the internet and succeeded in swapping it for bigger and better things. Twelve months and thirteen swaps later, he announced that his final deal had got him a property, a two-storey farmhouse in Kipling, Saskatchewan. **[1]** It certainly turned out to be more than that!

Kyle graduated with a degree in geography before travelling the world. He did odd jobs – from delivering pizzas to working on oil rigs. One day he received an email from an old friend reminding him of a game called *Bigger and Better*, which they had played as children. In this game, you started with small objects and competed to see what you could trade them for. MacDonald finished reading the email, <u>glanced</u> down at his desk and saw a paper clip. **[2]** And so a strange and brilliant idea was born.

He wrote down this ambition: 'I'm going to keep trading up until I get a house.' His first offer was a pen in the shape of a fish. This was soon exchanged for a doorknob with a smiley face and the doorknob, in turn, for an outdoor stove. **[3]** It was, he says, 'just a great way to meet new people'.

In this, he did have some help. His father, an enthusiastic inventor, had come up with a new idea for restaurant tables. MacDonald travelled across America and Canada to advertise his father's product. On the way, he would stop off to meet the people who'd contacted him on his website and who he wanted to do business with on his paper clip project. **[4]**

As news of the website spread, MacDonald had to choose between hundreds of offers for each item he advertised, but he says their financial value was <u>irrelevant</u>. **[5]** Kyle continued to trade up. His trades included an appearance on TV, some time in a recording studio, an afternoon with the rock star Alice Cooper and a small role in a film. Finally, he got his house.

Kyle tries to explain his success. 'People might think this is an <u>odd</u> way to spend your time but remember that before money was invented, people swapped things for centuries. **[6]**

What's that blue plastic object on my desk? It's the top of an old pen. Once I might have thrown it in the bin but now I pick it up and turn it thoughtfully in my fingers. Today it's just a plastic pen top; tomorrow it could be a villa in Tuscany!

Grammar

be/get used to ▶ CB page 54

1 Complete the text with the correct form of *be used to* or *get used to*.

I'm from Spain and I came to live in the UK a few months ago. I'm a shopaholic and I love shopping, but it's taken me a while to **(1)** .... shopping here. I live in a village and the shops close at 5.30 p.m. I **(2)** .... that because in Spain they're open much later and I **(3)** .... being able to go shopping after work. I can't do that now, so I have to either shop online or wait until the weekend.

Another thing I **(4)** .... is the prices because they're much higher in the UK. I think it might take me ages to **(5)** .... shopping without comparing how much I'd spend on a similar item back home. The sizes are different too, so I can't just walk into a shop and pick something up without trying it like I **(6)** ....!

2 Find and correct the mistakes in the sentences.

1 I still haven't got used to get up so early for my new job.

2 Sue didn't think she'd like living on her own but she used to it now.

3 I got used to do all my shopping online when I moved to a small village a long way from any big shops.

4 Antonio says it's too difficult to be used to the British weather, so he's going back to Portugal.

5 Jen didn't used to getting so much attention from the media. It's all new to her and she hates it.

6 It took me ages to be used to living in a big city but I love it now.

Use of English

Multiple-choice cloze ▶ CB page 55

1 Match the words (1–6) to the parts of speech (A–F).

1 customer   **A** adjective
2 therefore   **B** adverb
3 quickly   **C** linking word
4 down   **D** preposition
5 expensive   **E** verb
6 spend   **F** noun

2 Read the article and decide which answer (A, B, C or D) best fits each gap.

🛒 Supermarket scams

Supermarkets are very **(0)** *A good* at deceiving their poor customers, it seems. Customers think they are getting good **(1)** .... for money but they aren't. They are **(2)** .... getting much less of a bargain than they imagine. Here are a couple of the most common tricks used by supermarkets to **(3)** .... their customers spending.

You might think that buying a bigger packet would cost you quite a lot **(4)** ...., right? Wrong. At Fas Mart, for example, a 100-g jar of coffee costs £3.00. A 200-g jar, **(5)** ...., costs £5.99 – a saving of only one penny!

Special offers. You've seen them on the shelves – 'buy one, get one free'. The best offers are usually on fruit and vegetables – but can you really eat all those potatoes before they **(6)** .... bad and you have to throw them **(7)** ....?

So, **(8)** .... to think about what you're really buying before you fill up your shopping trolley!

0	**A** good	**B** well	**C** fine	**D** right
1	**A** price	**B** value	**C** charge	**D** cost
2	**A** absolutely	**B** exactly	**C** actually	**D** correctly
3	**A** keep	**B** hold	**C** continue	**D** last
4	**A** less	**B** fewer	**C** lower	**D** slighter
5	**A** although	**B** whereas	**C** despite	**D** however
6	**A** get	**B** go	**C** become	**D** are
7	**A** A up	**B** around	**C** off	**D** away
8	**A** forget	**B** avoid	**C** remind	**D** remember

Writing
Essay ▶ CB page 56

1 **Read the statements about writing an essay and decide if they are true (T) or false (F).**

1 It is all right if you don't cover all the points in the exam task.

2 You don't need to include an introduction as long as the conclusion is clear.

3 It is a good idea to give examples or reasons for your point of view.

4 You don't need to worry about paragraphs as long as your points are clear.

5 Using linking words and phrases will make your essay easier to read.

2 **Read the exam task and complete the essay on the right with the words in the box.**

all	although	balance	clearly	other
however	point	seems	such as	true

In your English class you have been talking about money and happiness. Your teacher has now asked you to write an essay.

Does having a lot of money always make people happy?

Notes
Write about
1 health
2 security
3 .... (your own idea)

Write an essay using **all** the notes and giving reasons for your point of view. Write **140–190** words.

People often imagine that anyone who has a lot of money must be happy. But are they really?

First of (1) .... , I must say that (2) .... money can appear to make people happy, this may be an illusion. (3) .... , money can't buy good health, and that's crucial for happiness. What is the point of having money if you are not well enough to enjoy spending it?

On the (4) .... hand, having a lot of money can provide security for people and stop them worrying about a lot of things, (5) .... having somewhere to live. It (6) .... to me that this kind of security is also a kind of happiness.

Another (7) .... to consider is that if people have money, they can enjoy their free time because they can buy things like theatre tickets or foreign holidays. It is certainly (8) .... that entertainment like this does make people happy. (9) .... , it could also be said that helping other people is more satisfying.

On (10) .... , I think having a lot of money does make people happy, but it is not very meaningful unless they do something useful with it.

3 **Match the highlighted phrases in the essay to these phrases with a similar meaning (1–6).**

1 On the whole ....

2 Obviously ....

3 At the same time ....

4 As far as I'm concerned ....

5 To begin with ....

6 Nevertheless ....

4 **Read the exam task and make notes to plan your answer. Then write your answer.**

In your English class you have recently had a discussion about money. Your teacher has now asked you to write an essay.

Is it better to save money or to spend it?

Notes
Write about
1 enjoyment
2 security
3 .... (your own idea)

Write an essay using **all** the notes and giving reasons for your point of view. Write **140–190** words.

6 Working lives

Vocabulary

finding a job
▶ CB pages 58–59

1 Choose the correct option in italics to complete the sentences.

1 A job should give you *a sense/an emotion* of achievement that makes you feel that you've done well.

2 Ambitious people look for a job that has good *ambitions/prospects* so that they can advance quickly.

3 However much you love your job, I think you need to find a good work-life *balance/similarity* or you miss out on some important things.

4 I need a *fully-paid/well-paid* job because I have to pay a lot for my accommodation.

5 My mum gave up her *complete-time/full-time* job when she had a family and went *part-time/half-time* for several years.

6 Could you send me an *applying/application* form for the job advertised in the paper?

2 Match the words (1–8) to their meanings (A–H).

1	secure	**A**	not temporary
2	status	**B**	money for a job paid weekly
3	rewarding	**C**	not likely to change; that you can depend on
4	salary	**D**	a formal meeting for someone to ask you questions
5	stressful	**E**	money for a job usually paid every month
6	interview	**F**	important position
7	permanent	**G**	giving a lot of satisfaction
8	wage	**H**	causing a lot of worry

3 Complete the email with words from Activity 2.

Hi Brad,

I've really got to find a new job – one that's a bit less **(1)** .... than this one! I seem to be worrying all the time. Do you know of any job vacancies locally? I'm looking for something **(2)** .... – obviously, I want a job that I can depend on, at least for a few months. But it doesn't have to be **(3)** .... or long-term. Money isn't a big concern for me, so I don't need a high monthly **(4)** .... , but I'd really like to do something that's **(5)** .... and that motivates me. I had a(n) **(6)** .... for a job at a restaurant last week, but I haven't heard back from them. So any suggestions would be good!

Thanks!
Mick

Speaking
Collaborative task
▶ CB page 59

1 ▶ 11 **Read the questions and the exam task below. Listen to two students doing the task and answer the questions.**

1 Which point do the students NOT discuss?
2 Do they do everything they are asked in the task?
3 Which reason do they choose as the most influential?

Some people choose to do jobs that are considered to be dangerous. Here are some things they often think about. Talk to each other about what attracts some people to do dangerous jobs.

fewer qualifications required

high salaries

What attracts some people to do dangerous jobs?

dislike of routine

enjoying excitment

doing something unusual

Now decide which reason would make most people choose to do a dangerous job.

2 **Listen again and tick the comments the students make.**

1 Perhaps the salary isn't that important.
2 I'm afraid of being bored at work.
3 Jobs that have a routine are often boring.
4 Most people dislike working in an office.
5 Training is an important part of any job.
6 Some people love taking risks.

Discussion
▶ CB page 59

About the exam:
In Part 4, you will be asked some questions related to the topic of your Part 3 discussion. You will need to give your opinion. Sometimes you will be encouraged to give your opinion on a question your partner has answered, and you can always add to something they have said.

Strategy:
Try to give a full answer with your reasons and perhaps an example from your experience. You can add your opinion after your partner has answered and this can develop into a discussion.

3 **Match the questions (1–5) to the answers (A–E). Then complete the answers with the phrases in the box.**

it all	I've never thought	to think of it
that's an interesting		to be

1 Would you like to do a dangerous job?
2 Do you think it's a good idea for young people to do the same job as their parents?
3 Do you think schools should invite people who do dangerous jobs to talk to their students?
4 Some people say that people who do dangerous jobs should be paid a lot of money. Do you agree?
5 What do you think makes people do routine jobs?

A .... question. I'm not really sure. Some people should get paid more if the danger is very high and they're doing things to save people's lives. But if it's a choice – like a wildlife photographer – then no, not really.

B .... depends. Sometimes people see their parents doing a job that they love and they think, 'Yes, I'd like to do that too.' But not always.

C .... honest, I can't understand why some people choose to do boring jobs. I think they must have no ambition, and not really want to achieve anything special.

D .... about it before. I suppose it depends how much I needed the money! I couldn't see myself cooking in a hot kitchen, though!

E Come ...., that might be a good idea. I think children would enjoy listening to people like that at school. It would help them choose a good job too.

Reading
Multiple matching
▶ CB pages 60–61

1 You are going to read an article about people who turned their hobbies into jobs. Read the article quickly and decide if the statements are true (T) or false (F).

1 All the people are happy about what they have done.

2 All the people found it hard to turn their hobby into a job.

2 Read the article again. For questions 1–10, choose from the people (A–C). The people may be chosen more than once.

Which person

improved their skills in a new area quickly?	**1**
was uncertain about how attractive their product was?	**2**
made a decision not to do something they had planned?	**3**
found it difficult to build up their work?	**4**
did something they realised was wrong?	**5**
had a previous job they were not satisfied with?	**6**
has moved on from their first role in their new career?	**7**
was surprised that their hobby turned into a career?	**8**
developed a love for their work from someone else?	**9**
says they are lucky to have a satisfying career?	**10**

3 Match the underlined words/phrases in the article to their meanings (1–6).

1 try very hard to do something difficult ....

2 satisfactory ....

3 reaction ....

4 liked ....

5 became very interested in ....

6 someone with a lot of skill in a subject ....

How my hobby became my job

Three people tell features reporter Sue Carter how they turned their hobbies into full-time careers.

A Computer games inventor

When I was at school, I never used to pay attention in IT classes – not because I was bored but because I loved seeing what I could do on the computer. I'd play around on it when I was supposed to be doing my classwork. It was a bit naughty, I know, but it's how I came up with the idea for a new computer game. I got my friends to try it out at break times and they loved it. I wasn't sure whether other people would like it, though, so I decided to put it on a gaming site and see if I'd get any <u>response</u>. To my amazement, I did. People started messaging me about how much they liked it and suddenly everyone wanted to have a go. I couldn't believe that what started as me playing around at school became a real job, selling my game online. Eventually, I was developing games full-time and my new ones are becoming just as popular. I know some people <u>struggle</u> to find work that they enjoy, so I'm fortunate that my favourite hobby has also become my job.

B Jewellery maker

I've always <u>been into</u> making things. My grandma loved knitting and I remember watching her make tiny outfits for my dolls when I was young. Then, when I was a little older, she taught me to knit myself and there was no stopping me. I used to make crazy clothes that were the envy of all my friends. Then I started work in a busy office and didn't really have time to do what I loved most. Working in that office wasn't creative at all and I was disappointed not to be fulfilling that side of me. That's when I decided to learn something new and I went to a jewellery-making workshop. Immediately, I <u>was hooked</u> and I made loads of earrings and necklaces. I would give them to friends as gifts and it was my best friend, Nancy, who said I should try selling them. I set up a little online shop and got some good feedback from my new customers. It was slow to start with, and very hard work, but I've managed to establish a business that provides me with a <u>decent</u> income and I love my new job.

C Kite surfing instructor

I've spent my life in the water. I was first hired as a windsurfing instructor when I was eighteen, in the summer before going to university, just as a holiday job. They had just started offering kite surfing and I loved the idea of having a go at teaching it. I'd taught myself the summer before by getting out on the sea with a board and kite. Luckily for me, I picked it up straightaway. The sport became really popular at the centre and I loved my job so much that I made up my mind to stay on there full-time rather than go to university. I soon became an <u>expert</u> and found myself working on a water sports magazine as an editor and gave up teaching the sport. This meant I had plenty of free time to travel and try out new places to do kite surfing. I sometimes wonder what I'd be doing now if I'd gone to university, but I love what I do and there's no going back.

Grammar
making comparisons
▶ CB page 62

1 **Choose the correct option to complete the sentences.**

1 Sheila is *slower/more slow* than Lin but her work is more accurate.

2 Andula is a tree surgeon. She says it's *more dangerous/ the most dangerous* job she's ever had.

3 Charlie works the *longer/longest* hours of anyone I know.

4 Theresa has been *less/much* happier since she got a promotion.

5 Steven's job is *much more/most* stressful than mine.

6 Now that I've moved house, I don't have as far to travel to work *as/than* I used to.

2 **Complete the second sentence so that it has a similar meaning to the first. Use between three and five words.**

1 Megan's the best computer programmer in the department.

No one in the department .... as Megan at computer programming.

2 I've never read such an impressive application letter.

This is .... application letter I've ever read.

3 Jean is not as experienced as Rob in managing people.

Jean .... than Rob in managing people.

4 The old machinery wasn't very efficient but the new machinery is.

The new machinery is .... the old machinery.

5 He's a very fair boss – more so than any other I've had.

He's a .... than any other I've had.

6 I've never had such a bad job in my life.

This is .... I've ever had.

3 **Complete the dialogue with the comparative or superlative form of the adjectives in brackets.**

A: How are you enjoying your new job, Chris?

B: It's great, thanks. A lot of the people in my department are **(1)** .... (*old*) me and have worked for the company for a long time. They're **(2)** .... (*experienced*) me, which is good because I'm learning a lot from them. I'm starting to feel **(3)** .... (*confident*) in my role now.

A: That's good. Are your presentation skills improving too?

B: Yes! I gave my first presentation to new clients last week. It was **(4)** .... (*big*) group of people I've ever spoken to and it went really well.

Use of English
Open cloze
▶ CB page 63

1 Read the blog post quickly. Is the writer talking about a part-time summer job or voluntary work experience?

I'm having **(0)** _the_ best time in the Ecuadorian rainforest and I'm glad I decided to spend my gap year here before I go to university. I'm helping scientists protect the rainforest and the species of wildlife **(1)** .... live there. I work in a small team **(2)** .... other volunteers. We **(3)** .... research, collect data and help on construction projects. The first couple of weeks were tough **(4)** .... the climate and environment we're working in are very different from home. We had **(5)** .... do some training and we also learned first aid and other skills, which helped us to feel safer. The days are long and tiring but it's really rewarding to think I'm doing something so worthwhile. We don't get paid **(6)** .... we get our accommodation and meals for free. I've already learned loads **(7)** .... new stuff and the people I'm working with are cool. I'd love to come back **(8)** .... I've finished my studies!

2 Complete the blog post with one word in each gap.

Listening
Sentence completion
▶ CB page 64

1 ▶ 12 You will hear a woman called Zena Smith giving a presentation about her job as a stuntwoman. Listen and complete the sentences with a word or short phrase.

Zena Smith: My life as a stuntwoman

When Zena was a little girl, she particularly enjoyed watching **(1)** .... films.

Zena says that the first stuntpeople worked in **(2)** .... rather than action films.

Zena was encouraged to take part in a film by her **(3)** ....

Zena says that being good at activities like skiing or **(4)** .... can help to get work as a stuntperson.

Zena explains that becoming a stuntperson does not require formal qualifications, which she refers to as 'a(n) **(5)** .... '.

Zena says that working as a stuntperson is not **(6)** .... although people believe it is.

When Zena was a stunt double for a famous actress, she was lucky to be the same **(7)** .... and build as her.

Zena was thrilled when she was given a small **(8)** .... as a reward for her stunt work.

Grammar
obligation and necessity
▶ CB page 65

1 Choose the correct option in italics to complete the sentences.

1 I *don't have to/must* wear a uniform for my job. It's great because I can wear my jeans to work if I want to!

2 Peter *had to/didn't have to* leave home very early to get the train to work. He had a meeting at 8.30 a.m.

3 We *were supposed to/had to* move to the new offices today but they still aren't ready.

4 You *mustn't/don't need to* switch the computers off – I'll do it before I leave.

5 I think you *are supposed to/should* ask for a pay rise. Your salary hasn't increased for three years.

6 You *need to/mustn't* handle food without washing your hands first – it can be dangerous.

2 Complete the job advertisement with *have to*, *don't have to* or *mustn't*.

Market researcher required

This is a fantastic opportunity which you **(1)** .... miss! We are looking for an in-store market researcher to collect customer feedback on samples of our premier chocolate ranges.

Here's what the role involves:

- Placed in a variety of stores across the northwest, you will meet customers on a daily basis, so you will **(2)** .... dress smartly at all times.

- Talking to customers about their tastes is an essential part of this role, so you **(3)** .... be a friendly and sociable person.

- You will be part of a team of coworkers who will get together regularly to discuss and analyse customer feedback. Therefore, you **(4)** .... enjoy working with others to share your ideas.

- You **(5)** .... have a qualification in food science – none of our other researchers hold a degree. But you **(6)** .... be passionate about chocolate!

- You **(7)** .... send proof of qualifications at this point but if you think you've got what it takes, send your CV and covering letter to the address below.

Writing

email/letter of application
▶ CB page 66

About the exam:
In Part 2, one of the options may be a letter of application.

Strategy:
- Make sure you include all the information asked for in the question.
- Use a formal style.

---

1 Read the exam task and the letter below. What information from the task has the student NOT included?

> You see this advertisement in a local newspaper.
>
> ### Do you like working with children?
>
> We're looking for an enthusiastic play worker for children at our holiday club. Applicants must be qualified and motivated.
> Apply in writing, indicating your availability for interview to Ms G. Randall.
>
> Write your **letter** in **140–190** words in an appropriate style.

Hi Ms Randall,

I saw the job for a holiday club worker advertised in the newspaper last week and I want to apply for it. It seems to be something I would be suited for.

I believe I could do the job very well. I am currently working as an assistant nursery nurse and I really enjoy being with children. I am patient because I grew up in a family with a lot of children! I am enthusiastic and creative, and I love thinking up new games for children to play. Regarding my formal training, I have qualifications in child care and I also speak three languages: French, Italian and German.

My job finishes at the end of June, so I will be available for work over the summer. If you accept my application, I could start from 5 July. If you wish, I could send you references from two employers. I am enclosing my CV with my contact details.

What's the pay and what are the hours?

Please write soon.

Yours sincerely,
M. Benson
Maria Benson

2 Read the letter again and find four examples of language that is too informal. Can you think of more appropriate phrases?

3 Read the exam task and make notes to plan your answer. Then write your answer.

> You see this advertisement in a local newspaper.
>
> ### Want to work on a film?
>
> Over July and August, we will be filming a new adventure film in this area and we are looking for people to help with make-up and costume. Apply to James Deacon at Weekes Films, with details of your experience and availability.
>
> Write your **letter** in **140–190** words in an appropriate style.

7 Well-being

Speaking

Long turn ▶ CB page 70

1 Read the exam task and look at the photos below. Then read the comments (1–6). Which comments are relevant for Student A? Which comment is relevant for Student B?

> **Student A**, your pictures show people keeping fit in different ways. Compare the photos and say why you think the people have chosen to keep fit in these ways.
>
> **Student B**, which of these things would you prefer to do to keep fit? Why?

1 People often feel more relaxed when they're spending time with friends. ....

2 They are obviously taking some kind of class. ....

3 It must be quiet out in the countryside. ....

4 Like most people, I enjoy being out in the fresh air. ....

5 Music can help with exercise, so dancing is a good way of keeping fit. ....

2 ▶ 13 Complete a student's answer with the words in the box. Then listen and check.

as	look	maybe	must	other	perhaps	probably
see	seem	sure				

I like these pictures! It's good to see people who are keeping fit and enjoying themselves at the same time. Both the runners and the dancers **(1)** .... happy. Although the people in the first picture are training hard, they are also smiling; the dancers are smiling too. But the reasons they are keeping fit in these ways are **(2)** .... quite different. I mean, the runners are doing something physically hard, so you can **(3)** .... that they're concentrating on what they're doing. They **(4)** .... to be in a park or the countryside, so they're enjoying keeping fit away from all the problems involved in running in a city. The dancers, on the **(5)** .... hand, are inside. **(6)** .... it's a dance studio and this is a regular class. It looks **(7)** .... though they're enjoying the movements and the music. I'm **(8)** .... the dancers are happy because they're together and doing something they love as well as keeping fit. It **(9)** .... be very enjoyable for the people in both pictures to be able to do exercise they really enjoy, and **(10)** .... that's why they've chosen to keep fit in these ways.

Use of English
Word formation
▶ CB page 71

1 Add prefixes to make the negative form of the adjectives.

1 ....friendly   4 ....responsible
2 ....patient   5 ....lucky
3 ....loyal   6 ....complete

2 Choose the correct option in italics to complete the sentences.

1 The pharmacist was very *helpful/helpless* and gave me some drops for my eyes.

2 That was a very *thoughtful/thoughtless* thing to say. I feel upset now.

3 Laughter is one of the most *powerful/powerless* medicines. It makes you feel better.

4 Don't worry about the dog! He's completely *harmful/harmless*.

5 The information the nurse gave me about asthma was very *useless/useful*. I know what to do now.

6 What a *colourful/colourless* room. I love orange!

3 Read the article about what makes people happy. Use the word given in capitals at the end of some of the lines to form a word that fits in the gap in the same line.

What really makes people happy?

According to **(0)** *psychologists*, what really makes people happy might, at first, seem rather **(1)** .... Experts say that individual happiness levels are genetic, which is why some people manage to remain **(2)** .... even when things are going wrong, whereas others find it **(3)** .... to lift themselves out of a bad mood. But it's not all in the mind – actions count too. A certain amount of life **(4)** .... comes from spending time doing things we love. **(5)** .... which give us 'flow' – in other words, which keep us interested and focused – are **(6)** .... in helping us to forget our problems. Whether it's playing a **(7)** .... instrument or piloting a plane, the result is the same: doing things you're good at makes you feel better. Another thing that makes us feel happier is the **(8)** .... to forgive others, as well as doing things for people less fortunate than ourselves. So, let's get busy!

PSYCHOLOGY

EXPECT

HOPE

POSSIBLE

SATISFY

ACTIVE

EFFECT

MUSIC

ABLE

Vocabulary
health and fitness
▶ CB page 72

1 Read the clues and complete the crossword.

Across

1 You get this if you have an accident.

4 It's important to .... fit if you want to stay healthy.

7 People are taken to hospital in this.

9 A way of hurting your ankle.

10 You can get a lot of this in red meat – like steak.

Down

2 .... exercise helps the heart stay strong.

3 A doctor will give you the right .... for an illness.

5 This can help when you have a bad headache.

6 This is the best type of diet to have.

8 If your body is in good ...., you won't have so many health problems.

2 Complete the sentences with the correct form of words from Activity 1.

1 People who do a lot of exercise need a lot of .... in their diet.

2 I fell over during a football game and .... my ankle.

3 My aunt is over sixty but she's in good .... because she's always done a lot of exercise.

4 It isn't easy to .... fit if you're ill and in hospital.

5 My brother had a knee .... after a car accident and it took ages to get better.

6 For a .... diet, you should eat a little bit of everything.

3 Choose the correct option in italics to complete the sentences.

1 Apparently, there are a lot of health *profits/benefits* to drinking tea.

2 I went *down/out* with flu after staying with my cousin last week.

3 I've got a new cream to rub onto *hurt/aching* muscles. It's great after football.

4 My mum makes sure we all have a *balanced/fair* diet.

5 They say you can't *catch/take* a cold just from being in a low temperature.

6 How often do you work *up/out* in the gym?

7 Life *prediction/expectancy* is now something like eighty-five years for men.

8 It's hard to *keep/continue* fit if you don't have much time.

9 I've *taken/picked* up a stomach bug and I feel awful.

10 Knowing basic *first/best* aid can save lives.

Grammar
zero, first and second conditionals
▶ CB page 73

1 Choose the correct option in italics to complete the conditional sentences.

1 If *I'm/I'll be* hungry, I eat eggs because they fill me up.

2 What would you do if you *twist/twisted* your ankle?

3 *I'll/I'd* take a painkiller if I had a headache.

4 I'll give you that diet information if *you want/you'll want* it.

5 If I were you, *I'll/I'd* go to bed earlier.

6 What do you do if your muscles *ache/will ache* after exercise?

7 It would be better if you *eat/ate* fresh fruit instead of chocolate!

8 If you do more exercise, *you'll/you'd* feel stronger and more confident.

2 Complete the post and comments about exercising with the correct form of the verbs in brackets.

Tina123

I watched this fascinating programme last night about exercise. It said that if you did just three minutes of intense exercise a week, you **(1)** .... (get) huge health benefits. Apparently, doing quick bursts of exercise, where you run or cycle as hard as you can for less than a minute each time, is better than the gym. Experts say that if you exercise like this, it **(2)** .... (keep) you in shape, and it also makes you want to eat less – whereas exercising for longer makes you hungrier!

BusyBea

I **(3)** .... (be) really annoyed if this is true because I'm a personal trainer and my job depends on people employing me to help them do training workouts. I wouldn't get paid much if I only **(4)** .... (work) for three minutes with each customer!

Gino-L

Well, I guess if you **(5)** .... (be) a lazy person, this way of exercising sounds like a great idea. But just three minutes of exercise a week? That's ridiculous!

ZigZag

I work really long hours and don't have time to go to the gym. So, if this worked, I **(6)** .... (find) time to try it.

DanDan

If you **(7)** .... (not exercise), you get fat and that's a fact. But only doing three minutes a week? Doesn't sound enough to me.

FunnyMouse

Think of all the time you **(8)** .... (save) if this were true! Instead of being bored at the gym or jogging round the streets in the winter, you could be doing something more interesting, like seeing friends. Great idea!

Listening
Multiple matching
▶ CB page 74

1 ▶ 14 **Listen to four people talking about alternatives to seeing the doctor about health problems. Match the speakers (1–4) to the photos (A–D).**

A

B

C

D

2 **Listen again and choose from the list (A–F) what each speaker does. There are two extra letters which you do not need to use.**

A uses information to decide whether to get professional help

B seeks advice from strangers with similar experiences

C follows advice given by a member of the family

D likes to find out about modern advances in treatment

E tries to learn about unfamiliar medical problems

F always seeks medical help immediately

Speaker 1 ☐
Speaker 2 ☐
Speaker 3 ☐
Speaker 4 ☐

Grammar
unless, otherwise, provided that
▶ CB page 75

1 *Unless, otherwise* and *provided that* are used incorrectly in these sentences. Find and correct the mistakes.

1 Provided that this cough clears up soon, I'll go to the doctor's for a prescription.

2 I must stop eating so much, provided that I'll get fat.

3 You'll have health problems otherwise you eat healthily and take regular exercise.

4 Steve wants to be a nurse unless he passes his final exams.

5 If you want, I'll give you a lift to the hospital. Unless I'll see you later instead.

6 Jenny said she would help me with my exercise plan this week unless she has the time.

2 **Complete the article with *unless*, *otherwise* or *provided that*.**

Vitamins and minerals

Toni Sherry asks whether we really need to take supplements.

Open any health magazine and you'll see hundreds of adverts for vitamins and minerals. I've tried many of them, but I haven't noticed any real differences in my health. In fact, I think that **(1)** .... you have a particularly poor diet, you should get everything you need from what you eat. But am I right about this? I asked health expert Brian Peacock for advice.

'Yes, you're right,' he tells me. '**(2)** .... you stick to a healthy eating plan, you shouldn't need to take additional vitamins or minerals.
(3) .... your body is suffering from a lack of a particular vitamin and your doctor gives you a prescription for something, you should be fine –
(4) .... you could be taking more vitamins than your body actually needs.'

He goes on to tell me that beliefs have changed in the medical profession over the benefits of taking extra vitamins and minerals. '**(5)** .... you're pregnant, when taking folic acid is recommended, don't bother wasting your money. Buying vitamins from health food shops is expensive, so
(6) .... you've been specifically advised to take them, leave them on the shelf.'

Reading
Multiple choice
▶ CB pages 76–77

1 Read the article quickly and choose the best title.

A A project to learn from

B An unexpected success

C A way to improve your mood

2 Read the article again. For questions 1–6, choose the answer (A, B, C or D) which you think fits best according to the text.

1 Many elderly people today in care homes are unhappy because

  A they can't move as easily as they used to.

  B they don't interact much with the staff.

  C they don't see people from outside the care home.

  D they don't have anything interesting to do.

2 The social experiment described in the article involved elderly people

  A learning how to teach.

  B visiting a day care centre.

  C sharing activities with young children.

  D going for regular checks to monitor their health.

3 Some of the residents were

  A worried about joining in the physical games.

  B concerned about the children's possible reaction.

  C confused about the reason for the project.

  D unhappy about the children's behaviour.

4 The writer uses Hamish to give an example of

  A how the residents' physical health improved.

  B how the children changed some residents' attitude to the project.

  C how the games suited both children and residents.

  D how the project activities were organised.

5 One positive effect of the experiment was that the children

  A became more polite.

  B started to think more about other people.

  C communicated better with their parents.

  D improved their grades at school.

6 One consequence of the project could be that

  A the friendships will continue.

  B other countries will copy the example.

  C the nursery will repeat the project again next year.

  D future care homes will be built with nurseries attached.

What impact can a group of lively four-year-olds have on the lives of residents in a care home for the elderly? Will they be welcomed with open arms or will the old people see them as a noisy distraction from newspapers and the normal peace and calm? An amazing social experiment that brings the two generations together has been filmed for a TV series called *Old People's Home for Four-Year-Olds*. The results of the experiment are fascinating.

Social isolation is a big problem today. People are living longer because of improved healthcare and advances in medicine. However, many pensioners in care homes suffer from loneliness. Their physical well-being is looked after by the staff, but incredibly, it appears that nearly sixty percent of these residents never have any visitors. As a result, they suffer from depression and many never move from their chairs. They become weaker and less mobile, which can cause additional health problems.

In an attempt to improve the mental well-being of older people, a team of doctors and film-makers recently carried out an unusual social experiment. They brought together a group of pre-schoolers and a group of residents, by setting up a temporary nursery in a Bristol care home. They timetabled special activities for the two generations to do together. Doctors would carry out tests on the elderly group at various stages of the experiment, checking their physical and mental health. The question was: how co-operative would the participants be? And what effect would they have on each other?

Understandably, several of the pensioners were nervous. They had spent such a long time away from young children that they weren't sure how they should treat them. They worried that they might say the wrong thing or that the children wouldn't want to talk to them. Some weren't enthusiastic about participating. One elderly man, Hamish, was clearly unwilling to share his time with children. He liked his newspaper and insisted that he wouldn't leave his chair as he had problems walking.

The children, on the other hand, took no notice of any hesitations the pensioners might have, and from the start brought positivity and energy into the home. They refused to take no for an answer and immediately involved the old people in the planned activities. They sang songs together, did art projects, played games and even had a mini sports day. Storytelling in particular was a big favourite with both groups. The children also loved hearing about the pensioners' lives and learning about nature from them on walks round the grounds. Even Hamish stopped complaining and at one point was filmed lying on the floor pretending to be a lion!

The experiment continued every day for six weeks and tests showed that the effects on the two groups were remarkable. The old people's moods improved greatly and even their mobility was affected. Interacting with the young obviously benefitted them in many ways. In addition to this, children's parents reported benefits too. They grew in confidence and their communication skills improved. They also became more considerate and one parent mentioned how her four-year-old now said hello to every old person they saw while out shopping!

This experiment was probably the first in the UK but in other countries intergenerational projects like this have been going on for quite a while. In Seattle, USA, something similar started twenty-five years ago and there are many examples of successful nursery schools linked with the elderly in Japan. Here in Bristol the project ended with smiles and tears, and promises to keep in touch. But already there are other projects starting up in different areas, and even plans for a permanent nursery in a care home in London. With luck, this could be the way forward for many lonely, isolated elderly people in the future.

Writing
Informal email/letter
▶ CB page 79

1 Read the exam task. Underline the phrases in the email that show it is written in an informal style.

You have received an email from your Canadian friend Pam, who is revising for her end-of-year exams. Read this part of the email and write your email to Pam.

> I need some advice. I've got end-of-year exams next week and I'm having real problems revising! There seems so much to do and I can't concentrate! Help! Any ideas?
>
> Love,
> Pam

Write your email in **140–190** words in an appropriate style.

2 Here are some sentences from a reply. Which sentences are NOT relevant?

1 I'm not good at revising, either.
2 How did the exams go?
3 Make sure you take lots of breaks.
4 It's a good idea to plan a revision schedule.
5 Forget about it. Enjoy yourself!
6 It sometimes helps to work with a friend.
7 If you want to meet me for coffee, that would be great.
8 I find that I concentrate best in the evenings.

3 Complete the phrases with the words in the box.

about	don't	hear	idea	sorry
well				

1 It's good to .... that …
2 I'm .... to hear that.
3 Hope all goes ....!
4 That sounds like a great ....
5 Why .... you … ?
6 Or how .... … ?

4 Make notes to plan your own answer to the exam task in Activity 1. Then write your answer. Try to use phrases from Activity 3.

8 Nature study

Vocabulary
animals ▶ CB page 80

1 Choose one word in each group that does not fit.

1	reptile	insect	cat	mammal
2	feathers	wings	fur	scales
3	fins	paws	claws	fish
4	bear	crocodile	salmon	shark
5	dragonfly	owl	sr ake	kingfisher

2 Decide if statements 1–10 are true (T) or false (F).

1 Fish use their fins to breathe.
2 Kingfishers live in the water.
3 Bears have brown skin.
4 Owls have feathers.
5 Dragonflies use their paws to fly.

6 Salmon eat with their beaks.
7 Snakes don't have claws.
8 Reptiles can swim, crawl and fly.
9 Ants don't have wings.
10 Crocodiles are covered in fur.

Listening
Multiple choice ▶ CB page 81

About the exam:
In the exam, you listen to an interview or discussion between two speakers and answer seven multiple-choice questions. Each question has three options to choose from.

Strategy:
• Read the questions and options carefully so that you know what you need to listen for.
• You will hear the recording twice. If you are unsure of any answers, you can focus on these the second time you listen.

1 ▶ 15 Listen to part of a radio interview and answer the questions.

1 Who is Michelle? ....
2 Who is Rufus? ....

2 Listen again and choose the best answer, A, B or C.

1 How did Michelle feel when she first got Rufus?

  A worried that he might get bored

  B relieved that he behaved so well

  C surprised by how intelligent he was

2 What did Michelle find most difficult about training with Rufus?

  A learning to look after him properly

  B memorising what instructions to give him

  C remembering to give him time to run around

3 What does Michelle think is the biggest difference Rufus has made to her life?

  A She has made more friends.

  B She has become more independent.

  C She is more confident when she goes out.

4 Michelle thinks the guide dog trainers chose Rufus for her because

  A he likes being active.

  B he's a small animal.

  C he enjoys walking quickly.

5 What does Michelle say about taking Rufus to college?

  A She loves letting her friends play with him.

  B The attention he gets is difficult to deal with.

  C He cannot be with her all the time.

6 What does Michelle like most about Rufus?

  A He can be very funny.

  B He makes her feel better.

  C He gets on well with her family.

Grammar

the passive

▶ CB page 82

1 Complete the sentences with the correct passive form of the verbs in brackets.

1 Zoo animals .... (look after) very well these days.

2 My dog .... (see) by the vet at the moment.

3 The kitten .... (rescue) by the fire service when he got stuck up a tree.

4 The fences at the safari park .... (repair) soon.

5 I've just had a call from the stables to say my horse .... (steal)! I can't believe it!

6 The animal rescue centre .... (give) a large donation by a local charity last year.

2 Complete the text with the correct active or passive form of the verbs in brackets.

RUDYARD KIPLING'S

Just So Stories

Rudyard Kipling was a British author who wrote a series of stories for children called *Just So Stories*. These fabulous tales are a work of fantasy, in which strange things happen to animals and people. They **(1)** .... (*first/publish*) in 1902 and they describe how animals – in the writer's imagination – **(2)** .... (*change*) from their original form to how they appear today. Some changes **(3)** .... (*make*) by humans, while others happened magically.

In *How the Camel got his Hump*, the camel **(4)** .... (*give*) the hump on his back as a punishment for refusing to work, and in *The Sing-song of Old Man Kangaroo*, we find out how the kangaroo got his powerful back legs from **(5)** .... (*chase*) by a wild dog all day. The dog **(6)** .... (*send*) to chase the kangaroo after the kangaroo **(7)** .... (*ask*) to be made different from all other animals.

The original editions of the stories **(8)** .... (*illustrate*) by the author himself and they **(9)** .... (*still/enjoy*) by children and adults today. Editions of the stories **(10)** .... (*also/release*) on DVD so that people can watch them too.

Speaking
Collaborative task
▶ CB page 83

1 ▶ 16 **Listen and complete the examiner's instructions.**

Here are some things people can do to **(1)** .... the environment. Talk to each other about **(2)** .... these things can help the environment.

recycling rubbish

collecting rainwater

How can these things help the environment?

turning off lights

putting food out for birds

travelling by bike

Now decide which is the most **(3)** .... thing for everyone to do.

2 ▶ 17 **Complete the extract from a conversation between two students doing the task in Activity 1. Use the words in the box. Then listen and check.**

again   catch   follow   know
mean (×2)   saying   shall

A: So, we have to talk about how these things can protect the environment. **(1)** .... we start with 'recycling rubbish'?

B: OK. Well, obviously, recycling your rubbish is really important. It helps because then we don't put so much stuff into landfill sites.

A: What do you **(2)** .... 'landfill sites'?

B: That's what they call those great big rubbish dumps in the countryside. You **(3)** ...., the rubbish stays there for ages.

A: I get it. Yeah, we reuse things and don't have to use energy and new materials to make things from scratch.

B: You **(4)** ...., like clothes and things?

A: Exactly. What about putting out food for birds? Do you think that's a good thing to do?

B: Sorry, I didn't **(5)** .... that.

A: Do you think putting out food for birds is a good thing to do?

B: Well, yes. Because with climate change a lot of bird species are dying out.

A: Sorry, I don't **(6)** ....

B: What I mean is, sometimes the winters are harder and they can't find food; or the summers are hotter and they don't get enough water.

A: So, are you **(7)** .... that it's more important to feed birds than recycle rubbish?

B: No, I'm just pointing out that a lot of our wildlife is having a bad time and it's good to help, don't you agree?

A: Um, … could you say that **(8)** .... ?

B: It's good to help …

A: Sorry, I meant the bit about the wildlife.

3 **Match the examiner's questions (1–5) to the students' answers (A–E).**

1 Do you do any of these things or know someone who does?

2 Do you think governments should do more to help the environment?

3 Is the climate in your country changing a lot? How?

4 Should schools teach children about the environment when they are very young? Why/Why not?

5 Do you think it's too late for us to do anything about environmental problems? Why/Why not?

A Actually, it is. We get a lot more rain than we used to. Also, we've had some very cold winters recently.

B No. There's a lot we can do. The problem is that people don't like changing their habits!

C A friend of mine has bought an electric car but at the moment there aren't many places he can charge it! So, he can't travel very far.

D Definitely. That's because people like you and me can't do a lot on our own.

E I think so. In my country they do. And also even before they start. My young sister had some books about things like recycling before she started school.

Reading

Gapped text
▶ CB pages 84–85

1 Read an article about a famous conservationist who adopted a herd of elephants. What did he learn from the elephants?

2 Read the article again. Six sentences have been removed from the article. Choose from the sentences (A–G) the one which fits each gap. There is one extra sentence which you do not need to use.

A A few years later, when Anthony's first grandchild, Ethan, was born, he did the same.

B And not just a normal herd of elephants, but a notorious wild herd that had caused damage to huge areas of KwaZulu-Natal in South Africa.

C But also, he had no idea that a group of troublesome elephants would teach him a lot about family love and loyalty.

D In spite of this, the young elephants treat the older ones with respect and love.

E And one morning, instead of trying to get out, she just stood there.

F Every morning, the elephants would try to break out of the compound where they were living.

G Angry elephants can be very dangerous animals if they don't like you.

3 Complete the sentences with the underlined words in the article.

1 The animals have a _____ life when there is no rain for months.

2 Someone _____ the glass in the window to break into our house.

3 When my dad got a job on the nature magazine, it was a _____ in his career.

4 It's important for children to _____ their teachers.

5 The survey produced some _____ results that no one had predicted.

6 I'll _____ my parents to let me go on holiday to Africa with my best friend.

CONSERVATION

THE HERD INSTINCT

Several years ago, the conservationist Lawrence Anthony adopted seven wild elephants in South Africa.

Lawrence Anthony remembers the moment he met his ready-made family for the first time. 'They were a difficult group, no question about it,' he says. 'Very naughty. But I could see a lot of good in them too. They'd had a <u>tough</u> time and were all scared and yet they were looking after one another, trying to protect one another.'

From the way he talks, you might think that he was talking about problem children; in fact, it's a herd of elephants. **1** | Farmers were now threatening to shoot them. 'I was their only hope,' says Anthony, 59. 'There were seven of them in all, including babies and a teenage son. But the previous owner had had enough of them – they'd <u>smashed</u> their way through every fence he had.'

Anthony knew dealing with elephants like this was risky. **2** | But when an elephant welfare organisation spoke to him, Anthony, a respected conservationist, knew he couldn't refuse.

Today he says that he had never imagined the job would be so hard. 'It's been 100 times harder than I'd thought,' he says. **3** | 'The care these elephants have for each other is <u>astounding</u>,' he says. From the start, Anthony considered the elephants part of his family. 'We called the oldest mother Nana because that's what all the children in the Anthony family call my mum,' he says.

As with human adoptions, the early days were especially difficult. **4** | Every day, Anthony, like many parents who have to deal with difficult kids, would try to persuade them not to behave badly. 'I'd go down to the fence and I'd <u>beg</u> Nana not to break it down,' he says. 'I knew she didn't understand English, but I hoped she'd understand by the tone of my voice and my body language what I was saying. **5** | Then she put her trunk through the fence towards me. I knew she wanted to touch me – elephants are tremendously tactile; they use touch all the time to show concern and love. That was a <u>turning point</u>.'

Today, the Anthonys are so close to their elephants that occasionally they have almost had to chase them out of the sitting room! Anthony has always believed that if he respected them, they would <u>respect</u> him. When Nana's son, Mvula, was born, she brought the baby to Anthony. She wanted to show him to the man who she now considered part of her family. **6** | 'Mind you,' he says with a laugh, 'my daughter-in-law didn't talk to me for a long time afterwards. There I was, holding her tiny baby, walking towards a herd of wild elephants. The elephants were so excited – their trunks went straight up and they all came closer, completely focused on the little child in my arms, sniffing the air to get the smell. I was trusting them with my baby, just as they had trusted me with theirs.'

Adopting a herd of wild elephants was probably the biggest risk Anthony ever took, but it worked. He is now as much a part of their family as they are of his.

Grammar

causative *have*

▶ CB page 86

1 Rewrite the sentences using the causative *have*.

Example:

We built a new shed for our garden tools.

We had a new shed built for our garden tools.

1 We have made our garden into a habitat for butterflies.

We .... into a habitat for butterflies.

2 We've replaced our old windows with double glazing.

We .... with double glazing.

3 We installed a solar panel on our roof.

We .... on our roof.

4 We fitted some curtains that keep in the heat.

We .... that keep in the heat.

5 We're going to make some of our lawn into a vegetable patch.

We .... into a vegetable patch.

6 We replaced our coal fire with a wood burner.

We .... with a wood burner.

Use of English

key word transformation

▶ CB page 87

1 Complete the sentences with the prepositions in the box.

for	of (×3)	on (×2)	up	with

1 I think it's important to protect the environment .... to a point, but we shouldn't worry too much.

2 Poor little dog! He's in desperate need .... a drink after that long walk in the heat.

3 We should take advantage .... new energy-saving devices.

4 Local residents are .... bad terms with the council for not collecting their rubbish.

5 I didn't drop litter .... purpose – the paper just fell out of my pocket!

6 Climate change isn't going to be good .... many animals.

7 I'm afraid you can't use the snack machine – it's out .... order.

8 There's no point in getting annoyed .... me. There's nothing I can do to change things!

2 Complete the second sentence so that it has a similar meaning to the first sentence, using the word given. Do not change the word given. You must use between two and five words, including the word given.

1 Someone at the car wash washed Terry's car.

HAD

Terry .... at the car wash.

2 I'm sorry, I didn't mean to break the window – it was an accident.

PURPOSE

I'm sorry, I didn't .... – it was an accident.

3 The hurricane caused a lot of damage to buildings around the city.

BY

A lot of damage .... to buildings around the city.

4 The town council have decided to provide more recycling bins next year.

BE

More recycling bins .... the council next year.

5 I've noticed changes in the weather over the last few years.

BEEN

There .... in the weather over the last few years that I've noticed.

6 I'm not sure about the idea of keeping a pet dog in a busy town.

WHETHER

I don't know .... good idea to keep a pet dog in a busy town.

7 It is necessary to find new ways to reduce our energy usage.

NEED

We .... new ways to reduce our energy usage.

8 We can reduce air pollution by using electric cars.

BE

Air pollution .... by using electric cars.

Writing
Article
▶ CB page 88

About the exam:
In Part 2, one of the options may be an article. This is usually for a magazine, newspaper or website. An article should be interesting for the reader and should include opinions and comments.

Strategy:
- Try to use a catchy title and interest the reader by asking a rhetorical question.
- It's good to add some humour and you can use an informal style.
- Remember to divide your article into clear paragraphs.

1 **Read the exam task below. Which points do you think the writer should NOT include?**

1 whether it's good to keep these animals in captivity

2 how many animals there are left

3 a detailed description of a campaign to save the animal

4 reasons for the animal's problems

5 the writer's own opinion about the situation

6 examples of animals around the world that are facing the same problems

You have seen this notice in an international nature magazine.

Animals in danger!
Write an article about an endangered animal in your area or country, saying why it is endangered and how you feel about it. We will publish the best three articles in next month's magazine.

Write your **article** in **140–190** words in an appropriate style.

2 **Read the article and check your ideas.**

Sadly missed!
There's an animal that I really love and sadly, it is disappearing from our area. It's a very pretty and clever animal that used to be found all over the UK. Now it can only be seen in a few protected places, such as the Isle of Wight and some parts of Scotland. This animal is the red squirrel.

Why is this beautiful animal disappearing? Are humans destroying its habitat? Are we hunting it for food? Is it perhaps because of the changing climate? The answer to all these questions is no! Red squirrels are dying out because of an invader. Grey squirrels, not native to the UK, somehow crossed the Atlantic from northern American in the nineteenth century. Because they are bigger and stronger than the red squirrels, they take all the food and the red squirrels can't survive in the same area. The greys are pushing them out!

This is a real shame. Unfortunately, we are losing many animal and plant species because of unwanted invaders like these from other parts of the world. Perhaps people should not be the only ones to have passports and security checks when they enter the country!

3 **Read the article again and answer the questions.**

1 Which animal is the article about? ....

2 Why is it endangered? ....

3 What is the writer's opinion? ....

4 **Find these words in the article that show the writer's use of a range of vocabulary.**

1 two adverbs that show the writer's opinion ....

2 three adjectives to describe the red squirrels ....

3 two adjectives to describe the grey squirrels ....

4 two phrasal verbs ....

5 a verb that means 'manage to stay alive' ....

6 a noun that means 'the place where an animal lives' ....

7 a noun that means 'an uninvited visitor who takes over the land' ....

8 a phrase that means 'it's a pity' ....

5 **Are these alternatives for parts of the article better than those used by the writer?**

1 Title: The Red Squirrel

2 Opening sentence: The red squirrel is a beautiful animal which cannot be seen very often in our area today.

3 Opening – second paragraph: The red squirrel is not in danger because of climate change or because humans are destroying its habitat.

4 Opening – final paragraph: There are many animals disappearing.

6 **Make notes to plan your own answer to the exam task in Activity 1. Then write your answer.**

9 Future society

Listening
Sentence completion ▶ CB page 90

1 ▶ 18 **You will hear a girl called Ana Williams talking about her visit to an exhibition. Listen and answer the questions.**

1 What kind of exhibition did Ana visit?

2 Which of these rooms in the exhibition does she NOT mention?
- transport
- fashion
- art
- robots
- communication
- games
- fitness

2 **Listen again and complete the sentences with a word or short phrase.**

An exhibition of virtual reality, technology and innovation

Ana says that the advertising for the exhibition referred to it as a **(1)** ...., which she thought was an exaggeration.

Ana uses the word **(2)** .... to refer to what she thought of the exhibition.

In the fitness room, Ana tried equipment that checked the user's performance as well as their general **(3)** ....

In the fashion room, Ana found clothes that changed colour based on people's **(4)** .... the most surprising.

In the games room, Ana wondered whether any of the **(5)** .... made by visitors would be taken up by technicians.

Ana found her conversation with a robot **(6)** .... after a while.

In the art room, Ana was surprised to find that virtual reality can promote **(7)** ....

Ana says that some structures in the art room changed **(8)** .... when visitors came in large numbers.

Ana was glad that **(9)** .... was considered important in car innovations.

According to Ana, it was interesting be able to compare things mentioned in **(10)** .... with real life.

Vocabulary
computers ▶ CB page 91

1 **Choose the correct option in italics to complete the sentences.**

1 It's annoying when someone *hacks/enters* into your social media account.

2 I always organise my desktop *figures/icons* in alphabetical order.

3 It took ages to install the new *software/passwords* on my computer.

4 You shouldn't *click/scroll* on some email attachments in case they contain viruses.

5 Some areas of the country have no broadband *indication/signal* at all.

2 Complete the sentences with the correct form of the words in the box.

---
bring   click   freeze   identity   menu
recognition   reset   stream   upgrade
---

1 Voice _____ would be a great step forward in making computers more user-friendly.

2 You should _____ on 'File' and _____ up the drop-down _____.

3 _____ theft is a potential security risk online, so you should _____ all passwords regularly.

4 You should _____ your operating system regularly and run the latest version.

5 Which websites do you use to download music and _____ films?

6 I hate it when my laptop just _____ and I can't do anything.

Grammar

future perfect and continuous
▶ CB page 92

1 Choose the correct option in italics to complete the sentences.

1 There's no way we'll *be living/have lived* on the moon any time soon.

2 I'm so pleased John will *be making/have made* dinner by the time I get home. He said it will be on the table waiting, so I won't have to cook.

3 At this time tomorrow I'll *be swimming/have swum* in the hotel pool. It'll be great!

4 I'm going to make sure my son will *be learning/have learned* the alphabet by the time he goes to school. He'll know all the letters.

5 I'm in so much debt I'll *be paying/have paid* it off till I'm sixty!

6 I hope we'll all *be using/have used* renewable energy in the near future – that is, before our natural resources run out.

7 David will *be going/have gone* to the tennis club when he finishes his homework.

8 The council will *be spending/have spent* its entire budget by the end of summer. They'll have nothing left.

9 If all goes well, my sister will *be finishing/have finished* her degree by June.

10 Mark will *be going/have gone* to bed by the time we get back.

2 Complete the dialogue with the future continuous or future perfect form of the verbs in brackets.

A: What do you think you **(1)** _____ (*do*) this time next year?

B: Well, by then I **(2)** _____ (*finish*) my final exams, so I think I **(3)** _____ (*celebrate*)! I **(4)** _____ (*enjoy*) my holiday and I **(5)** _____ (*sunbathe*) on a beach somewhere hot. What about you?

A: Well, I've just finished my own studies, so I hope by next June I **(6)** _____ (*find*) a decent job. If I'm lucky, I **(7)** _____ (*earn*) lots of money and I **(8)** _____ (*buy*) myself a car!

B: Fingers crossed, then!

Speaking

Long turn
▶ CB page 93

1 Look at the photos below and complete the extracts from some students' answers with the words in the box.

---
call   exact   gone   remember   thing
---

1 He's wearing a … – what do you _____ it? When the jacket and trousers are the same?

2 He's standing on the … – I can't _____ the word. It's where you wait for a train.

3 The girl is wearing … – sorry, I don't know the _____ word.

4 It's the _____ businesspeople keep papers in.

5 The girl might be watching a cartoon film or a … – sorry, it's _____.

2 Match the words (A–D) to sentences 1–4 in Activity 1.

A earphones   B suit   C briefcase   D platform

3 Read the exam task below and two students' answers. Match these comments (1–4) to the answers (A–B). Which answer is better?

1 This answer only describes the photos.
2 This answer says how the people are feeling.
3 This answer says why the people are using technology.
4 This answer compares the photos.

Your photos show people using technology while they are travelling. Compare the photos and say why you think the people are using the technology.

A The man in the first picture is at a station. It looks as if he is waiting for an underground train because I can't see any trees or any sky. I think he looks like a businessman because he's wearing a suit. He isn't wearing a tie though. He is carrying a briefcase and he is holding a tablet. In the second picture, I think the girl is on a train. She's sitting by the window and she's looking at a laptop. She's possibly watching a film or talking to a friend. She has long hair and she's wearing a ribbon in her hair. I think it's summer because she's wearing short sleeves.

B The people in both pictures are travelling. The man on the platform is waiting for a train, whereas the girl is already on the train. The man at the station looks like a businessman; he's got a briefcase and he's wearing a suit, and he's using his tablet while he's waiting. He might be reading his emails and planning his day. The girl, on the other hand, is probably just killing time while she's travelling. She's probably watching a film or talking to a friend. Neither of the people look very stressed and I think they are both using technology to make their day or their journey easier and more enjoyable.

4 Read the follow-up question. Which is the best answer?

Do you often use technology when you're travelling?

A I find it hard to concentrate when I'm travelling, so I don't usually use my laptop or tablet. But I do listen to music on my phone.

B I travel by bus and it's quite uncomfortable plus it stops all the time. I like talking to my friends when I travel.

Reading
Multiple choice
▶ CB pages 94–95

1 Read the questions and the article. Underline the parts of the article where you think the answer to each question is.

1 In the first paragraph, the writer says that
   A films that are made today reflect modern society.
   B science fiction films weren't very good in the past.
   C old sci-fi films are amusing to watch.
   D some old films guessed the future correctly.

2 When talking about *Forbidden Planet*, the writer makes the point that
   A the characters in the film were the first to use modern mobiles.
   B it is unfortunate that the film's predictions didn't come true.
   C the film made predictions that didn't come true for a long time.
   D the film helped to bring about the progress of technology.

3 What does the writer say when talking about *The Truman Show*?
   A It was unlike any other film that had been made about reality TV.
   B Its main character was unaware of the role he was playing.
   C People are more interested in celebrities than they should be.
   D At the time it wasn't easy to become famous.

4 What does *observes* mean in line 38?
   A wants   B notices   C cares   D ignores

5 When talking about *Minority Report*, the writer says that
   A we are already experiencing similar technology to that seen in the film.
   B the main character is confused by what he sees in the shopping centre.
   C it is likely that all the film's predictions will come true.
   D he doesn't like being exploited by advertising companies.

6 In the final paragraph, the writer expresses the opinion that
   A we are all worried about what will happen in the future.
   B we are unlikely to do certain things that have been suggested.
   C we will continue to see inventive ideas in films.
   D we are eager to believe the fantasies we are sold in films.

2 Read the article again and answer the questions in Activity 1. Choose the answer (A, B, C or D) which you think fits best according to the text.

Films that predicted the future

As humans, we are obsessed with the future and this is reflected in films which predict what future society and technology will be like. It's easy enough to laugh at old sci-fi films but many contained details which proved to be an accurate prediction of life to come. Let's take a quick look at one or two from past decades.

Forbidden Planet, a science fiction film released in 1956, was the first film that was set in space and was one of the first of the modern sci-fi films that predicted life in the future. The film's characters were shown using handheld 'communicators' that they would carry everywhere with them, much like we do with our mobile phones today. This was one prediction that came well ahead of its time – it took another forty years before the use of mobile phones became widespread.

line 38

In 1998, when *The Truman Show* was released, there were very few TV reality shows around. This film follows the life of insurance salesman Truman Burbank, who does not at first realise that he is the focus of a reality TV show broadcast to millions of people around the world. These days, TV is full of such shows, and while – unlike Truman – the people involved agree to take part in them, the shows reflect society's current fascination with celebrity. It might have been an interesting idea to make a film about someone's day-to-day life in 1998, but these days we can't turn on the TV without seeing yet another weird and wonderful version of reality on shows on nearly every channel.

Another sci-fi film, this time from this century, is *Minority Report*, which came out in 2002. While most of the film's predictions haven't come true (yet), in one scene of this popular film, the main character is seen walking through a shopping mall where his eyes are scanned by 3D screens. As he looks around him, he observes that the adverts he sees on the screens are directly aimed at him – screens even call his name to attract his attention, which they eventually get. It's certainly a strange scene but aren't we nearly there? Think about when you use the internet to search for something. If you often look up books, for example, you soon start seeing adverts pop up on your screen for new titles because your computer saves your searches. The film was actually set in 2054, so perhaps by then some of the film's other predictions, like crimes being prevented before they happen, might have come true.

Have we seen it all now? I doubt it. Interested as we are in technological advances and our own personal futures, I'm sure there is plenty yet to come from the imaginative minds of sci-fi scriptwriters. And perhaps living on the moon isn't as far away as we think.

Grammar
reported speech
▶ CB page 96

1 **Rewrite the sentences in reported speech.**

1 'As humans, we are obsessed with the future,' said sci-fi director Ken Smithies.

....

2 'It took forty years before the use of mobile phones became widespread,' he said.

....

3 'TV reality shows reflect society's fascination with celebrity,' said the reporter.

....

4 'Most of the film's predictions haven't come true yet,' Ken reported.

....

5 'Do we really want to mess with our minds?' the scientist asked.

....

6 'I'm sure there is still plenty to come from the imagination of scriptwriters,' she told me.

....

2 **Read Meg's post on the right about students' hopes for the future and complete this text using reported speech.**

Meg said she **(1)** .... (*do*) a survey about what students at her college hoped to do in the future. She said she **(2)** .... (*interview*) fifty people so far.

Judie said she **(3)** .... (*take*) ballet classes since she was five but she had grown too tall to become a professional dancer. She said she **(4)** .... (*be*) a dance teacher instead. Michel said he had been asked to sign for a professional football team and he **(5)** .... (*start*) training with them soon. Sonia said she **(6)** .... (*not know*) exactly what she wanted to do, but was thinking about becoming a dentist. Jared said he **(7)** .... (*be*) really into rock climbing and he hoped to make that his career. Linda said she **(8)** .... (*be*) on work experience in an airport and thought being an air traffic controller **(9)** .... (*be*) exciting.

Meg promised to put the full survey on the college website once she **(10)** .... (*collate*) the results.

I'm doing a survey about what students at my school hope to do in the future. So far, I've interviewed fifty people. Here's what a few of them said.

Judie, 14: 'I've been taking ballet classes since I was five and I've always wanted to be a professional dancer. The problem is I've grown too tall to become a professional dancer, so I'm going to be a dance teacher instead.'

Michel, 15: 'I'm going to be a footballer. I've already been asked to sign for a professional youth team and I'll start training soon!'

Sonia, 13: 'I don't know exactly what I want to do yet, but I'm thinking of becoming a dentist.'

Jared, 16: 'I'm really into rock climbing, so I hope to make that my career!'

Linda, 19: 'I've just been on work experience at an airport and I'd love to be an air traffic controller. How exciting would that be?'

I'll put my full survey on the college website once I've collated the results – don't forget to take a look!
Meg

3 **Report these comments from three more students.**

Liz: 'I'm planning to take my final exams and then go to college. I'd really like to study art history.'

Jim: 'I've always wanted to be an actor! I'll probably stay at drama school for a couple more years and then audition for parts on television.'

Ian: 'My dream is to be a racing driver. I've been doing a lot of karting recently and I've won a lot of races, so maybe one day my dream will come true!'

1 ....
....

2 ....
....

3 ....
....

Use of English
Open cloze
▶ CB page 97

1 You are going to read an article about food in space. Scan the text. Which two of these problems with food are mentioned?

1 storing   **2** seasoning   **3** cooking

Food in space
What'll be on the menu?

In future we may have to consider **(0)** _the_ possibility of living on other planets. Does this sound far-fetched? The concept itself may not be, but the distances involved in travelling to **(1)** _____ and the provisions required for the journey will be problematic. Consider the amount of food you'd need for only **(2)** _____ few days' camping, and then multiply this by years. You'll also **(3)** _____ to plan how to keep the food safely so that it won't **(4)** _____ gone off when you want to eat it, and where to dispose of any leftovers!

Long-distance travellers in space will certainly **(5)** _____ eating some food in its normal form, **(6)** _____ as biscuits, although they will be adding water to create meals like pot noodles or porridge. Of **(7)** _____, any travellers will want to enjoy the taste of their food, so salt and pepper will be vital. Unfortunately, these **(8)** _____ have been turned into liquids – you can't have small particles of pepper floating around a spaceship!

2 Complete the article with one word in each gap.

Writing
Report
▶ CB page 98

1 Read the exam task and complete the report on the right with the words in the box.

aim	although	appears	expected
number	percent	said	worth

You have been doing a survey at your college about ways students use their computers. Now you have been asked to write a report for your teacher. In your report, you should explain the results of your survey and draw conclusions from them. Write your **report** in **140–190** words in an appropriate style.

Introduction
The **(1)** _____ of this report is to outline how students at our college use their computers and analyse the results.

Students' use of computers
Research
A large **(2)** _____ of the students go online to do research for their homework and special projects. Most students **(3)** _____ that they spend several hours a day on their computers for this reason.

Communication
Most students use email or online video software every day to contact friends or family. By far the most popular form of communication seems to be via social networking sites, **(4)** _____ this is usually done in the evenings rather than in college.

Games _a survey at_
Fewer students than **(5)** _____ play computer games regularly. A small number play for an hour or more every day. About fifty **(6)** _____ seem to play for a few hours at the weekends. Just one or two students said that this was their main use of the computer.

Conclusion
It **(7)** _____ from the results that computers are commonly used for study-related activities, although social networking is a top priority for most. It may be **(8)** _____ carrying out another survey during holiday time to compare the results.

2 Match the highlighted phrases in the report to these phrases with a similar meaning.

1 It might be useful to …
2 This report is intended to …
3 The results seem to show that …
4 A lot of …
5 According to the majority of students, …
6 Almost half …

3 Read the exam task and make notes to plan your answer. Then write your answer.

You have been doing a survey at your college to find out what students use their mobile phones for. Now you have been asked to write a report for the college magazine. In your report, you should explain the results of your survey and draw conclusions from them. Write your **report** in **140–190** words in an appropriate style.

10 Global culture

Reading
Multiple matching
▶ CB pages 102–103

1 Read the article quickly and decide if the statements are true (T) or false (F).

1 All the people went to theatrical performances.
2 Their favourite performers were all male.

2 Read the article again. For questions 1–10, choose from the people (A–D). The people may be chosen more than once.

Which person

had not expected to enjoy the performance?	1
watched a performance of something made famous by another person?	2
was concerned about their reaction to the performance?	3
prefers the theatre to the cinema?	4
watched a performance of fictional events?	5
was reminded of a family member?	6
appreciates more than one form of entertainment?	7
enjoys the preparations before going to see a show?	8
has a different opinion to many others about a particular form of entertainment?	9
found a large part of the performance amusing?	10

3 Complete the sentences with the correct form of the underlined words/phrases in the article.

1 At the end of the show, I _____ so hard that my hands hurt!
2 I _____ the main actor. He was incredible.
3 I wouldn't advise anyone to _____ that film. It was terrible.
4 Everyone _____ loudly when the singer won the prize.
5 It's nice to _____ to go to a party or a show.
6 The actor only played a small part but he later _____ to become a famous film star in Hollywood.

4 Match the highlighted adjectives in the article to their meanings (1–6).

1 not real _____
2 extremely sad _____
3 having a strong effect on your feelings or opinions _____
4 unforgettable _____
5 very excited or happy _____
6 excellent _____

A memorable performance

A Donna

I love going out to the theatre and I enjoy all types of shows, from comedy to musicals and dramas. It's the whole thing – getting dressed up and looking forward to it. Also, it's brilliant being part of an audience. You can feel the atmosphere and see how different people react to what's on the stage. Live performances are so much better than film or TV for me. I think one of the best performances I've ever seen was during a play called *Shadowlands*. The play is about C.S. Lewis, the man who wrote the Narnia books – you know, *The Lion, the Witch and the Wardrobe*? He fell in love with an American poet called Joy Gresham but she died quite young and he was heartbroken. Both the main characters were wonderful but the actress playing Joy was superb.

B Martin

I was only a teenager – about fourteen, I think – when I went with the family to see the musical *Les Misérables* in London. It's set at a particular time in France but the story is imaginary. The show was part of a day trip and we'd spent the morning going round the sights, so we were pretty tired by mid-afternoon, which is when we saw the performance. It was a matinée but the theatre was completely full. I wasn't exactly thrilled about going as I wasn't particularly into the theatre at that time, but that performance really changed my opinion. It was magnificent! From the opening moments of the show to the final song, I couldn't take my eyes off the stage. I've been back to see it again and again since then. I was particularly impressed by the male singer who was the male lead, Jean Valjean – his voice was amazingly powerful. And at the end everyone stood up and clapped and cheered for ages.

C Kelly

A lot of people think that TV talent shows don't really produce good singers but I definitely don't agree. I always choose my favourite and then I vote for them every Saturday! A couple of years back, my favourite was a young male singer called Tom Barker. I remember he wore a hat and looked a bit like my cousin, Billy. I thought he had a great voice. He went on to win the TV show, which was great. Then, for a surprise Christmas present, my mum paid for me and my best friend to go to see the singers from the show when they went on tour. Tom sang *The First Time Ever I Saw your Face*, a song that Roberta Flack had sung a long time ago, and I cried. I'll never forget how much it moved me.

D Mark

It sounds odd but one of the most memorable performances I've seen wasn't by a person but a dog! It was a film made from a book I had read, called *It's Bailey!* It was a real story about a teenage girl who gets a dog that is really naughty. Most of the book is very funny but the ending is really sad. When they made the film, I knew I had to see it but I was a bit worried about how I'd feel at the end. Well, the film was good, mostly very funny and with some clever dog acting, but at the end the dog playing Bailey was perfect. I'm not a very sensitive person and I don't normally cry at the end of sad films, but I did with this one. I don't believe anyone could sit through that film and not cry. It's impossible.

Grammar
relative clauses
▶ CB page 104

1 Complete the sentences with *who*, *which*, *where*, *when* or *whose*.

1 That's the woman .... asked me for directions. She's lost.

2 She's the girl .... dog ran into our garden.

3 This is the map .... will show you where your hotel is.

4 I suppose I could see you at seven, but that's the time .... I'm normally having dinner.

5 That's the hotel .... we stayed on our honeymoon.

6 This is the book .... I bought for Sue.

2 Complete the article with *who*, *which*, *that*, *where*, *when* or *whose*.

La Tomatina

Many of us have heard of La Tomatina, the tomato-throwing festival **(1)** .... *is held in Spain each summer. But what really goes on there? Reporter Sue King tells us more.*

La Tomatina is a celebration **(2)** .... people take part in the world's largest tomato fight. It takes place on the last Wednesday of August, **(3)** .... it starts with the *palo jamón*. The aim of this fun activity is to climb to the top of a pole **(4)** .... is covered in slippery grease. The leg of ham on top is the prize for the person **(5)** .... can reach it without sliding back down the pole or falling off. When someone finally grabs the ham, the tomato fight begins. Trucks full of tomatoes to be thrown at the crowd enter the town square. These tomatoes come from an area of Spain called Extremadura, **(6)** .... they are grown specifically for the festival. The estimated number of tomatoes **(7)** .... are used in the fight is around 150,000. After exactly one hour, **(8)** .... shots are fired from water cannons, the fight ends. The square **(9)** .... the fight has taken place is then washed down and the participants, **(10)** .... bodies and faces are now covered in tomato paste, are also provided with water to clean themselves up. See you there next year?!

Speaking
Discussion
▶ CB page 105

1 Read the discussion questions (1–4) and the students' answers below (A–B). Which question is each pair of students answering?

1 Fewer people read books these days. Why do you think this is?

2 How important do you think it is to read stories to a young child? Why?

3 When there's a film based on a book, is it better to see the film first or read the book? Why?

4 Many people read e-books these days. Do you think this is a good thing? Why/Why not?

Discussion A

A: OK, let me think. You know, I'm not really sure. Sometimes, **(1)** .... me, it's better to read the book first. That's **(2)** .... I get my own pictures in my head about the characters. What **(3)** .... you?

B: Yes, I like to read the book. The **(4)** .... is that a book is not only about what happens – the story or plot; it's the way it's written, how the writer makes us imagine the pictures. A film is different.

A: I agree. **(5)** .... why I don't understand people who say, 'It wasn't as good as the book.' I'm not sure we should compare them because they're different.

B: Mhm. Take, for **(6)** ...., the *Harry Potter* books and films. They're classics now and still popular. Children still read and love the books, but they get pleasure from the films for different reasons.

A: You know, in my **(7)** ...., that's a special example. **(8)** .... you think that the books and films sort of lead into each other?

B: Yeah. That's a good point.

Discussion B

A: I feel **(1)** .... that it is very important for parents to read to their children. It helps their imaginations to grow. My mum would read to me every night and I looked forward to it a lot. **(2)** .... do you feel about this?

B: I couldn't agree more. It also helps the relationship between parent and child. I **(3)** .... that because sometimes it's the only time in the day that they have the chance to have time together. But you're right. It helps children in so many ways. **(4)** .... instance, my dad used to read me adventure stories **(5)** .... *The Time Machine* and *Treasure Hunt*, and I loved them so much I couldn't wait to learn to read myself.

2 ▶ 19 **Complete the discussions in Activity 1 with the words in the box. Listen and check.**

about	because	don't	example
for (×2)	how	like	opinion	reason
say	strongly	that's		

3 **Underline words/phrases in the discussions in Activity 1 that are used to**

1 ask for an opinion.
2 give an opinion.
3 give a reason.
4 give an example.
5 talk about experiences.

Listening
Multiple choice: short extracts
▶ CB page 106

1 ▶ 20 **You will hear people talking in eight different situations. For questions 1–8, choose the best answer, A, B or C.**

1 You hear a man and a woman talking about a play. How does the man feel about it?
   A sorry that he has missed the opening night
   B upset that his friend didn't tell him about it
   C concerned that he needs to book a ticket in advance

2 You hear two friends talking about a television programme. What was it about?
   A a hotel
   B an old film
   C an art exhibition

3 You hear some travel information on the radio. What does the presenter warn people about?
   A There are delays to flights from Bournemouth.
   B There is a lot of traffic going to a car festival.
   C Drivers won't be able to use one of the roads.

4 You hear a man and a woman talking about a meal they had together. Why did the man feel unwell?
   A He ate too much.
   B He was allergic to the food.
   C The meal he chose was badly cooked.

5 You hear a man leaving a voicemail message. Why is he leaving the message?
   A to make a suggestion
   B to make a request
   C to make an arrangement

6 You hear a man and a woman talking about a sculpture exhibition. How does the woman feel about it?
   A She regrets not going to it.
   B She is pleased it was in her home town.
   C She dislikes the style of the main artist.

7 You hear a man and a woman talking about English books. What type of book is the man going to recommend to his friend?
   A a children's book
   B a book for English learners
   C a detective novel

8 You hear a man talking about buying books online. What problem did he have when buying online?
   A His receipt was incorrect.
   B He was sent the wrong book.
   C A book arrived in bad condition.

Vocabulary
arts and culture
▶ CB page 107

1 **Read the clues and complete the puzzle. What's the hidden word?**

1 the lines of a play
2 a large group of people playing instruments
3 a long written story
4 practice for a play or concert
5 one of the parts of a book
6 a person who plays music
7 a person in a book, film or play
8 a person who paints pictures
9 a person who directs people playing music
10 when actors compete to get a part in a film, play, etc.
11 the story of a book, film or play
12 actors need to learn these for a play or film

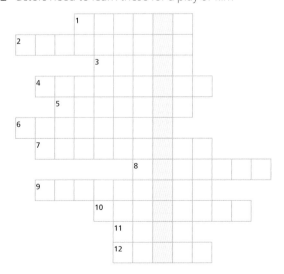

2 Complete the sentences with the correct form of words from Activity 1.

1 I've lost my _____ for the new play we're doing in drama club. Can I borrow yours?

2 The _____ of the film is very complicated.I got really confused towards the end.

3 Our school _____ is going to play in a concert on TV next month.

4 I read the first three _____ of the book but then I got bored and didn't finish it.

5 The main _____ in *Romeo and Juliet* are from two families.

6 Dorothy Sayers wrote excellent detective _____ .

7 Janet is a very talented _____ . She plays the violin beautifully.

8 We've had five _____ for the play but I still don't know all my _____ .

Grammar
articles
▶ CB page 108

1 Complete the sentences with *a*, *an*, *the* or – (no article).

1 Tina's going to live in _____ Monte Carlo for _____ year and she's really looking forward to it.

2 I saw _____ brilliant film last night!

3 Sue had _____ headache yesterday, so she didn't go to Mick's party. _____ party was great fun, so it's a pity she missed it.

4 Hotpot is _____ dish from _____ North West England made from _____ potatoes and _____ lamb.

5 I'm not usually into _____ football but _____ match I saw last night was really exciting.

6 Dan's going to _____ North Pole next summer – how exciting is that?

7 That's _____ best play I've ever seen.

8 The town's annual music festival will be held in _____ Brown Street this year.

9 This is third time Stacy's been to _____ Scotland. She's from _____ USA and she loves it here.

10 Jim's _____ instructor at _____ golf course; he's very good.

2 Complete the blog post with *a*, *an*, *the* or – (no article).

British FOOD

I'm English and I get a bit frustrated with the ideas people from other countries have about British food.

Lots of visitors to **(1)** _____ England end up going to fast food restaurants or eat in cheap places where **(2)** _____ food isn't particularly good and then complain about it. I admit that in the past our meals weren't very exciting – lots of meat and potatoes or greasy fish and chips. But these days we eat cuisine from all over **(3)** _____ world. I bet you didn't know that one of **(4)** _____ most popular meals in Britain now is actually **(5)** _____ dish called Tikka Masala from **(6)** _____ India! It contains lots of tasty ingredients like **(7)** _____ cream, spices and chicken. Italian food is popular too – you don't have to go far to find **(8)** _____ excellent restaurant serving up everything from **(9)** _____ pasta to seafood. But there are one or two traditional English meals that even people who aren't British love. How can you beat **(10)** _____ big plateful of bacon, eggs, sausages, beans and tomatoes for breakfast or some delicious roast beef for lunch?

Use of English
Multiple-choice cloze
▶ CB page 109

1 Choose the correct option in italics to complete the sentences.

1 I *did/made* so many mistakes in my German homework that my teacher said I had to *do/make* it again.

2 Jed's *done/made* a lot of money by working really hard. He's really *doing/making* his best in his job.

3 I *did/made* Ahmed a favour by *doing/making* his project for him.

4 Sarah dislikes Peter because he's always *doing/making* trouble. I told her to *do/make* an excuse and walk away whenever he tries to talk to her.

5 You've got to *do/make* the most of whatever difficult situation you find yourself in. There's no point just *doing/making* a wish and hoping that any problems will go away.

6 The people outside were *doing/making* so much noise that I couldn't *do/make* my homework properly.

2 Read the article. For questions 1–8, decide which answer (A, B, C or D), fits each gap.

Breaking a leg is good luck!

Well, that's what they say in the theatre, at **(0)** _A least_. Actors often wish each other good luck by saying 'Break a leg!' before they go on stage, **(1)** .... on opening nights. They believe that it's bad luck to say 'Good luck,' but no one really knows why!

Another theatrical superstition – a belief that a certain action will **(2)** .... in something bad happening – is that actors should not **(3)** .... 'the Scottish play' – Shakespeare's *Macbeth*. Actors are **(4)** .... that something unpleasant will happen if they say the name of the play in the theatre. There are several possible **(5)** .... for this superstition. One is that there are a lot of sword **(6)** .... in the play – and the more they are practised, the more **(7)** .... it is there will be an injury. Another **(8)** .... is that the actor who was going to play Macbeth in the first ever performance died shortly before it began.

0	A least	B last	C once	D most
1	A really	B totally	C completely	D especially
2	A start	B produce	C result	D cause
3	A mention	B observe	C notice	D tell
4	A believed	B influenced	C convinced	D proved
5	A stories	B explanations	C accounts	D reports
6	A plays	B arguments	C struggles	D fights
7	A likely	B possibly	C suitably	D clearly
8	A instruction	B method	C practice	D suggestion

Writing
Article
▶ CB page 110

1 Read the exam task and the article on the right. Tick the things the student has done.

The student has
1 organised the article into paragraphs.
2 included an introduction and conclusion.
3 used a title, to interest the reader.
4 written in a formal style.
5 given reasons and/or examples to support opinions.
6 used a range of vocabulary.
7 exceeded the word limit.
8 included rhetorical questions to engage the reader.

You have seen this announcement in an international magazine.

Articles wanted!
We are going to publish a series of articles about great writers or artists from around the world. Who is your favourite writer, painter, musician, etc.? Send us your article telling us about your favourite person and explaining why you like them. We'll include the best articles in the series.

Write your article in **140–190** words in an appropriate style.

An easy choice!

I know I should opt for an artist from my own country – and we've got plenty to choose from. But I'm going to be different and go for a writer from another country, who I think was the best writer in the world: William Shakespeare.

As everyone must know, Shakespeare was English. He lived in the sixteenth century and wrote many plays and poems during his lifetime. We don't know much about his life but his work is read, performed and studied all over the world. Everyone has heard his name, haven't they?

There are several reasons I have chosen Shakespeare. Firstly, although he wrote a long time ago, his plays are still relevant now. We can still learn from them. Secondly, he gave the English language a vast number of words and phrases that are still used today.

Finally, what I find amazing is that people from so many different cultures love and perform Shakespeare. He seems to speak to all people from all backgrounds, and that is why he is my favourite writer. I never get tired of his plays!

2 Read the article again. Find and underline
1 one rhetorical question.
2 three linking words used to sequence ideas.
3 two verbs that mean 'choose'.

3 Make notes to plan your own answer to the exam task in Activity 1. Then write your answer. Try to include all the points you ticked in Activity 1.

11 Style and design

Listening
Multiple matching ▶ CB page 112

1 ▶ 21 **Listen to five people talking about moving to a new home. Which speakers live in a house and which in a flat?**

2 Listen again and choose from the list (A–H) what each speaker dislikes about his/her new home. There are three extra letters which you do not need to use.

A the modern heating system   Speaker 1 ☐
B the lack of storage space   Speaker 2 ☐
C the floor covering   Speaker 3 ☐
D the small garden   Speaker 4 ☐
E the modern gadgets   Speaker 5 ☐
F the view
G the countryside surroundings
H the lack of privacy

Vocabulary
fashion and design ▶ CB page 113

1 Choose one word in each group that does not fit.

1	baggy	fitted	leather	short-sleeved	tight
2	cotton	fur	plain	silk	velvet
3	checked	flowery	loose	spotted	striped

2 Choose the correct option in italics to complete the sentences.

1 This shirt is too *tight/loose*. I can hardly breathe!
2 You'll need a *silk/leather* jacket if you go on Jim's motorbike.
3 I used to wear red and white *plain/striped* pyjamas when I was a child.
4 I don't like the *material/shape* of this dress – it's too thin.
5 In the hot weather you'll need to have some *fitted/short-sleeved* T-shirts.
6 People in cold countries often wear *cotton/fur* clothes to keep warm.

3 Put the adjectives in brackets in the correct order to complete the sentences.

1 The bride wore a _____,' _____,' _____ (white, silk, long) wedding dress.

2 My mum hated my new _____,' _____,' _____ (leather, tight, black) trousers.

3 We used to have some horrible _____,' _____,' _____ (velvet, floor-length, purple) curtains in our old house.

4 In the play I had to wear a _____,' _____,' _____ (cotton, checked, short-sleeved) cowboy shirt.

5 My dad gave me a _____,' _____,' _____ (silk, plain, blue) tie to wear to the interview.

4 Complete the sentences with the words in the box.

classic   conscious   designer   fake
fashionable   genuine

1 My aunt likes to be _____ and spends a lot of money on trendy clothes.

2 It that a _____ Mulberry bag? It must have cost a lot.

3 For kids today, the _____ name is more important than the look. They spend a lot of money on clothes.

4 My dad isn't very fashion _____ – he still wears clothes he bought when he was a teenager!

5 They're not made of real fur, don't worry. They're _____.

6 The design of that suit is a real _____ – it will never go out of fashion.

Grammar
modals of possibility and certainty
▶ CB page 114

1 Match the sentences (1–8) to the responses on the right (A–H). Then choose the correct option in italics to complete the responses.

1 Steffi has written a book about fashion, even though she studied science.

2 Whenever I wear this top, I get a nasty rash.

3 Is Henry always so rude to people he doesn't know?

4 I didn't get a place on the fashion course I wanted.

5 I've been calling the museum all day but nobody ever answers!

6 I can't find my ticket to the fashion show anywhere.

7 Gemma's been filming a make-up commercial since 6.30 this morning.

8 Look at the price of these boots – £500!

A You might *leave/have left* it in the kitchen. I think I saw it there earlier.

B Well, they *might/can't* be closed. Have you checked the opening times?

C Poor you! You *must/can't* be so disappointed.

D She must *be/have been* exhausted.

E She *must/can't* know a lot about the subject then!

F That *must/can't* be right – they must have made a mistake!

G You must *be/have been* allergic to the material.

H Not usually. You must *see/have seen* him on a bad day.

2 Complete the email with *must, can't* or *might* and the correct form of the verbs in brackets.

Hi Jim,

How are you? I've been really busy. My college organised a fashion show last week to raise money for charity. It was great fun. It **(1)** _____ *(take)* ages for the fashion students to make all the clothes. And the music department **(2)** _____ *(work)* really hard to create the music they put together for it. They asked me to be one of their models, which was great fun. They **(3)** _____ *(care)* much about what people looked like because I'm nothing like a model! But it was cool to be asked, and everyone who joined in did really well, so the organisers **(4)** _____ *(feel)* really proud.

The only disadvantage was that I wore my favourite shoes but I don't know where they are now! I **(5)** _____ *(leave)* them in the changing rooms at college or maybe at a friend's house – I stayed there afterwards.

The college **(6)** _____ *(expect)* so many people to turn up on the night because there weren't enough chairs in the hall and loads of people had to stand at the back to watch. They sold everything, though, and raised a few hundred pounds – well, it **(7)** _____ *(be)* a thousand, I'm not sure. Anyway, they **(8)** _____ *(make)* so much money at a college event before!

I really enjoyed being part of the show and I hope we do another one soon!

Write back and tell me all your news!

Mark

Use of English
Word formation
▶ CB page 115

1 Add suffixes to the words in the box to form nouns and adjectives. Write the words you form in the correct group.

able	account	appear	celebrate	contest
dark	dirt	educate	fit	flexible	hunger
insure	mass	offend		

1 -ance ....

2 -ion ....

3 -y ....

4 -ive ....

5 -ness ....

6 -ity ....

7 -ant ....

2 Read the blog post. Use the word given in capitals at the end of some of the lines to form a word that fits in the gap in the same line.

My (bad) experience of a **TV** talent show

Last year I was a **(0)** participant in a TV talent show called *You Got It!* I was excited about **PARTICIPATE**

entering the **(1)** .... and turned up for **COMPETE**

the auditions at a local theatre. **(2)** ...., **FORTUNE**

the judges loved what I did – I'm an acrobat –
and they invited me back for the next round.

But as I left the stage, I was **(3)** .... **SUDDEN**

surrounded by the contestants who hadn't got

through. I couldn't believe how **(4)** .... **OFFEND**

they were! I got nasty comments from them and

they made lots of **(5)** .... that I was **SUGGEST**

no good. It wasn't very nice but I didn't want it to

put me off. **(6)** ...., I passed the next **LUCK**

audition too and went on to show the public my

act on live TV. My **(7)** .... was going **PERFORM**

well until I slipped on stage and hurt my ankle and

that was the end of it. It was a **(8)** .... **DISAPPOINT**

but I'm going to try again next year.

Reading
Gapped text
▶ CB pages 116–117

1 Read the article quickly. How does the writer feel about her old park?

A regretful that it has lost its previous atmosphere

B concerned about the cost of the changes

C convinced that the changes were necessary

2 Read the article again. Six sentences have been removed from the article. Choose from the sentences (A–G) the one which fits each gap (1–6). There is one extra sentence which you do not need to use.

A I'm not saying that adults could climb into the wooden house or have a great time on the roundabout!

B For a start, I visit my local park regularly, sometimes with family, sometimes with friends and sometimes alone.

C This is just what the Victorians wanted to avoid by giving free access to everyone.

D It brings children together rather than separating them, and encourages creative play and adventure.

E Since then green spaces, big and small, have been important in the design of new building developments.

F On the other hand, these costs have increased dramatically.

G It was clean, beautiful and full of people.

3 Match the underlined words in the article to their meanings (1–8).

1 news that might or might not be true

....

2 very modern ....

3 talked about other people ....

4 annoyed or bored ....

5 a way of entering a place ....

6 benefit ....

7 valuable, important ....

8 strange ....

Change for the better

What would we do without city and town parks? They give us a space away from the noise and pollution of the streets where we can relax and pretend we're in the country for a while. It was the Victorians who realised that working people needed free <u>access</u> to quiet, green areas. **1** However, the way we use these <u>precious</u> areas has changed a great deal over the years.

For my parents, going to the park – usually on a Sunday after lunch – was a very different experience than it is now for me. **2** Back then the park was a place to walk through on your way somewhere or a place to send the kids to play while the parents were busy or <u>fed up</u> with them. A Sunday walk was an opportunity for some fresh air and to walk off dinner! At that time parks had trees, some flowers, paths and lots of grass where teenagers could kick a football around or catch up with their mates. I remember there were a couple of swings and a slide (which I fell off once and broke my arm!) and a sand pit where very young children got dirty while their mums sat and <u>gossiped</u> with their friends. There was litter on the grass and in the bushes, and graffiti all over the play equipment. In the evenings it was a dangerous place to be.

It's very different today. Safety and environmental issues have meant big changes to park design over the years. And in addition to this, park managers need to consider – and here's the buzz word – inclusivity. Parks everywhere must be welcoming places for all people, where everyone, no matter what their age, can come to <u>profit</u> from different activities. In other words, there is something for everyone. I could hardly recognise my old park when I returned last year. **3**

The sand pit has gone, unsurprisingly, as it used to be a source of cut glass and smelly, buried rubbish, but there is still a playground for the children. However, the equipment today is <u>state-of-the-art</u>! There's a wooden house that combines swings, a slide, ropes and balancing walls. **4** And there are other things there too, like the roundabout, which has access for wheelchairs, so children of all abilities can use it. Getting hurt on park play equipment was a normal event when I was young, but today the risks are greatly reduced by the soft, spongy material that carpets the play areas. It feels <u>odd</u> to me, but if it had been there when I was a child, I wouldn't have broken that arm!

Something else that impressed me was that the play equipment wasn't only for the children. **5** No, there's a green gym there, right beside the kids' play area. Teenagers and adults can work out on the ski-walkers, exercise bikes and pull-up bars. What a great idea – being able to keep fit in a lovely outdoor environment without paying expensive gym membership fees! And young mums and dads (even grandparents, I guess) can use the machines while watching their children play.

I think we're really lucky to have parks designed like these today. I've heard <u>rumours</u> that because of cuts in public spending, parks in the future may need to charge entrance fees. **6** Let's hope we can continue to do the same.

Grammar

so, such, very, too, enough
▶ CB page 118

1 Choose the correct option in italics to complete the sentences.

1 Wow! That was amazing! I've never seen *so/such* a good exhibition.

2 We're having our house designed by an award-winning architect – it's *so/such* expensive we'll be paying for it until we retire!

3 There was a huge storm last night and all the lights went out at home. It was *so/such* dark we had to light candles.

4 I've broken your favourite mug. I'm *so/such* sorry! I'll buy you a new one.

5 It's *so/such* an interesting programme – you have to see it!

6 Denzel's been offered a place at university – he's done *so/such* well in his exams!

7 There was *so/such* excitement in the crowd outside the hotel – you just knew that someone really famous was about to turn up.

8 I'd love to study art and design at college, but it's just *so/such* hard to make a living when you graduate.

2 Complete the sentences about a design exhibition with *very*, *too* or *enough*.

1 The furniture designs were _____ futuristic. I wouldn't mind having a piece in my home.

2 There weren't _____ toilets in the venue – maybe you should choose another place next time!

3 I usually like looking at photos but there were _____ many in this exhibition and you had to walk through them all to get to the next room.

4 My kids were _____ pleased with the toy section – I'm bringing them again next time!

5 Great office furniture – I'd order some but it's _____ expensive.

6 I didn't really enjoy this event – it was _____ boring compared with last year's exhibition!

7 The place was certainly big _____ to hold an exhibition like this, but it was cold and not very inviting.

8 We had to stand up to eat our lunch – there weren't _____ places to sit in the café. Great show, though.

Speaking

Long turn
▶ CB page 119

1 ▶ 22 Read the exam task and look at the photos below. Choose the correct options in italics to complete the student's answer. Then listen and check.

> Your photos show people designing different things. Compare the photos and say what you think the people are enjoying about designing these things.

Both pictures show people designing things, but they are completely different. The man in the first picture is designing something like a building, so I **(1)** *guess/say* he's an architect. The design looks very complicated – I **(2)** *imagine/sure* he's concentrating very hard. The woman is also concentrating very hard, but she is **(3)** *likely/obviously* designing clothes, not buildings – she **(4)** *can/could* be creating a new fashion! I'm **(5)** *sure/would say* the architect has a lot of responsibility to get things right, while the fashion designer is creating a new look that **(6)** *must/could* make her a lot of money. Both of them **(7)** *must /are probably* be enjoying their work – it's very satisfying to create something new. **(8)** *I guess/I'll think* the man gets a lot of pleasure from seeing his buildings in real life because it's very difficult work – **(9)** *I'll/I'd* say that makes him feel very proud. And the fashion designer **(10)** *must/probably* enjoys the fact that other people love wearing her clothes, and that she's making other people feel happy.

2 Read the follow-up question and three students' answers. Find and circle two extra words in each answer.

> Which of these jobs would you prefer to do?

1 I'd prefer for to be the architect. It might be fun that to design buildings for a living.

2 I would actually prefer to be a fashion designer because of I think it must be very interesting and I love to shopping for clothes.

3 I'm not completely sure, but I'm guess the architect could be doing a more useful job. I'm not so interested in fashion – it can be a little bit the boring. I would be proud to be an architect, so that's what I'd probably go for.

3 Read the students' answers in Activity 3 again. Match the answers (1–3) to the examiner's comments (A–C).

A This answer is rather short, although it does answer the question.

B This answer is a good length and gives a clear, interesting explanation for what the student thinks, with a reason.

C This answer is a satisfactory length, but it has some irrelevant information.

Writing

Review

▶ CB page 120

1 Read the exam task below and the review on the right and answer these questions.

1 What is the exhibition of?

2 Where is it?

3 What does it show exactly?

4 Why was it interesting for the writer?

> You have seen this notice on an international student website.
>
> If you have recently been to an interesting fashion or design exhibition, we would like to hear from you. Write a review of the exhibition, telling us about what you saw there and what you thought about it. We'll post the best reviews on our site.
>
> Write your review in **140–190** words in an appropriate style.

Don't miss this!

I'm studying art and design and I'm **(1)** .... interested in furniture. For this **(2)** ...., my parents took me to a fantastic exhibition of furniture in London last month. It was at the Living Design Museum and it shows how furniture has developed over the last 100 years.

You can see pieces of furniture from the early 1900s up to the present day. One of my **(3)** .... was a sofa by Salvador Dali shaped like a pair of lips! There is also a fascinating **(4)** .... of pieces that we may be using in the future. For me, it was very interesting to see **(5)** .... the designs have changed according to people's tastes and I wanted to look at every piece and every design carefully. **(6)** ...., the exhibition is far too big to see in just a few hours. I can **(7)** .... recommend this exhibition to anyone who, like me, is interested in art and design. Make sure you've got plenty of time though! It's only on for another four weeks, so my **(8)** .... is to get there soon.

2 Complete the review in Activity 1 with the words in the box.

advice	display	favourites	how
however	particularly	reason	thoroughly

3 Read the review again and decide which tip the writer has NOT followed.

1 Write about a recent exhibition you have seen.

2 Divide your review into clear paragraphs.

3 Say what it was and why you went.

4 Explain what you can see at the exhibition.

5 Give your personal reaction.

6 Include a recommendation.

4 Make notes to plan your own answer to the examtask in Activity 1. Then write your answer. Try to use as many of the highlighted phrases as possible.

12 Science and discovery

Reading
Multiple matching
▶ CB pages 122–123

1 Read the article about young female scientists. Match the scientists (A–D) with their jobs or intended jobs (1–4).

1 engineer   ☐   3 astrophysicist   ☐

2 botanist   ☐   4 forensic scientist   ☐

2 Read the article again. For questions 1–10, choose from the people (A–D). The people may be chosen more than once.

Which scientist

changed her attitude towards science at school?	**1** ☐
once experimented on something that wasn't hers?	**2** ☐
has a job in the media?	**3** ☐
didn't get a lot of encouragement at school?	**4** ☐
became interested in a fictional TV story?	**5** ☐
considered several different jobs?	**6** ☐
followed a family trend?	**7** ☐
was influenced by an expert on television?	**8** ☐
chose to study something related to her free time interest?	**9** ☐
didn't do what her parents expected her to do?	**10** ☐

3 Match the phrasal verbs from the article (1–6) to their meanings (A–F).

1 work out   A separate into pieces

2 pick up   B manage to understand

3 drop out   C join different parts to make something

4 pull apart   D choose

5 put together   E win

6 go for   F leave university early

4 Complete the sentences with prepositions. Find the phrases in the article and check your answers.

1 I don't see much point .... getting to the party early because no one will arrive before 8.30.

2 I think everyone can learn from the film – it makes you see things .... a different way.

3 Our teacher is enthusiastic, committed and dedicated .... her students.

4 I thought I'd failed the test but much .... my amazement, I got the best marks in the class.

5 My dad has had a love .... motorbikes since he was a teenager.

6 A year after getting her degree in science, she went .... a different direction and pursued a career in music.

Scientists today

Four young female scientists talk about why they decided to follow a scientific path.

A Ruth

Today, I absolutely love science and I cannot imagine doing a job that wasn't related to it. However, that hasn't always been the case. When I was younger, I used to hate science lessons. Our science teacher was very clever and knowledgeable, but he wasn't much good with children and he wasn't a good motivator. For me, science was hard and I couldn't really see much point in studying it. Then I started watching an American TV drama series about forensics, where the scientists are like detectives and work out how a person died. I found that really interesting and started to see my science lessons in a different way. Now I'm studying forensic science at university and loving every minute of it!

B Gabriella

Both my parents are scientists and they work in research, developing new medicines and vaccines. They're completely dedicated to their work and this has obviously had an effect on their children. My elder brother won a science scholarship to go to a top university to study physics and since then he's picked up several prizes for things he has invented. I went in a different direction and found that I loved botany. I used to spend hours in our garden planting and growing strange flowers and trees. Now I give advice to gardeners and you can see me in my own TV show on Saturdays!

C Gemma

I liked a lot of different subjects at school and I was quite good at a wide range of things. So, it was hard to decide what I wanted to do as a career. First I wanted to teach geography, then I decided I didn't have enough patience to be a teacher. After that I decided to do a sports degree because I loved swimming. I didn't enjoy the course, so I dropped out and became a personal trainer. Then, much to everyone's amazement, I applied to university to do an engineering degree in motor sports! I'd had a love of fast cars since I passed my driving test, and driving cars was my big hobby in my late teens. It was a brilliant course. Now I work for one of the famous Formula 1 racing teams. It's a great life – a bit different to teaching geography!

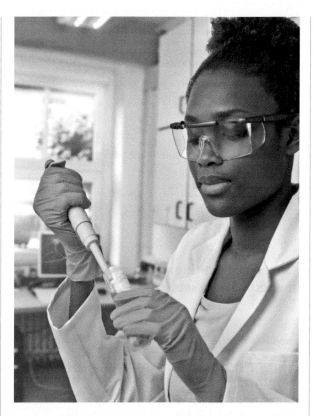

D Diana

When I was young, my mum and dad were convinced that I was going to be an engineer. Unlike other children, I wasn't interested in books and stories or even playing with toys. What I was interested in was pulling everything apart to see how it worked. The problem was that I never put them back together again and I think that through the years, I broke nearly everything I owned – and that other people owned too! I remember making my best friend cry because I took apart the new toy steam train that he'd just got for his birthday! So, it came as a surprise when I decided not to study engineering at university but to go for astrophysics instead! It's quite a long way from studying how things work to watching the stars and planets and learning all about what they're made of. But it all started when I saw the incredible scientist Brian Cox present a series of TV documentaries about the planets. He switched me on to the solar system and since then my head has literally been 'in the stars'!

Grammar
third conditional and *wish*
▶ CB page 124

1 Add one missing word in each sentence.

1 If no one invented the mobile phone, we wouldn't have been able to send text messages.

2 I have gone to the science museum with you if I had known you were going.

3 I wish I come up with an invention that had changed the world – I'd be famous now!

4 If my parents hadn't bought me a telescope, I wouldn't become so interested in the stars.

5 If Gary hadn't explained that experiment to me, I not have got a good mark in my physics homework.

6 I bet Toni wishes she gone to the talk – it was so interesting!

7 If they hadn't invented the wheel, we not have developed motor vehicles.

8 I wish I not dropped out of university because I would have a degree by now.

2 Complete the article with the correct form of the verbs in brackets.

Use of English
Key word transformation
▶ CB page 125

1 Choose the correct option in italics to complete the sentences.

1 An interesting topic *came up/fell through* in our debating club – we discussed animal conservation.

2 I'm finding it quite difficult to *look into/keep up with* my French evening classes. I don't understand the teacher very well.

3 The teacher *gave away/ran out of* the answers to the chemistry test by forgetting to cover them up, so everyone got them right!

4 I wish Tamsin wouldn't keep *going on about/coming up with* winning a prize for her design project – we know she did well!

5 The plans for a new sports centre *gave away/fell through* because they didn't get permission to build on the land.

6 I *came across/kept up with* my old school reports yesterday – I'd forgotten I still had them!

7 They had to return home from South America when their money *fell through/ran out*.

Thank goodness they invented it!
In a recent survey we asked people which inventions they were most grateful for. Here's what some of them said.

Mike, 25
Well, I **(1)** .... (get) lost dozens of times if they **(2)** .... (not invent) satnav for cars! I was never very good at using maps to find my way, so when I got a new car, I was so relieved that there was one built-in. I wish I **(3)** .... (get) one sooner because now I don't need to worry or ask anyone for directions. And as a bonus, there are parking sensors too!

Sarah, 17
Computer games! I don't play them myself but my friends spend a lot of time at their computers while I'm out playing hockey. I've just been accepted into a sports academy where I'm going to improve my skills. If no one **(4)** .... (come up with) computer games, perhaps I **(5)** .... (have) more competition from my friends on the sports field and I **(6)** .... (might/not get) in!

Tom, 19
No contest for me – it's contact lenses. I've never really minded wearing glasses in the past, but they can be annoying when it's raining. I got contacts last year and they're great, but if I **(7)** .... (buy) them sooner, I **(8)** .... (avoid) some rather embarrassing situations. One day I walked up to a girl who I thought was my sister and gave her a hug! Fortunately, she thought it was quite funny. In fact, she became a good friend. So, if I **(9)** .... (choose) to get contacts sooner, I **(10)** .... (miss) the chance of a good friendship!

2 Complete the second sentence so that it has a similar meaning to the first sentence, using the word given. Do not change the word given. You must use between two and five words, including the word given.

Example:

She managed to open the door.

IN

She succeeded in opening the door.

1 Jean told everyone about my idea for an invention.

AWAY

Jean .... my idea for an invention to everyone.

2 I didn't pass my science exam because I didn't work hard enough.

HARDER

If .... for my science exam, I would have passed.

3 Steph is always complaining about our new boss but I think he's OK.

GOING

Steph .... our new boss but I think he's OK.

4 I try hard to run at the same speed as everyone in the athletics team but I can't.

KEEP

I try hard to .... everyone in the athletics team but I can't.

5 Jack regrets not accepting Carla's invitation to her party.

WISHES

Jack .... Carla's invitation to her party.

6 Scientists will discover a cure for cancer very soon.

FOUND

Scientists .... a cure for cancer before very long.

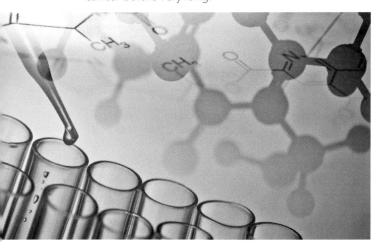

Listening
Multiple choice
▶ CB page 126

1 ▶ 23 **Listen to part of a radio interview. Who is speaking and what about?**

2 Listen again and choose the best answer, A, B or C.

1 Jamie became a science teacher because he
   A felt that science was based on magic.
   B particularly enjoyed the subject at school.
   C was inspired by his own science teacher.

2 What does Jamie like most about teaching science?
   A the materials he can use with his class
   B the interest that students have in the subject
   C the chance to see students find things out

3 What does Jamie say about teaching his favourite science subject?
   A It is difficult for many students to be good at.
   B The experiments are exciting to carry out.
   C It focuses on things that are easily recognisable.

4 What does Jamie find most difficult about teaching?
   A seeing students struggle to understand things
   B experiencing bad behaviour in class
   C not having the right material in class

5 How does Jamie feel about his school's entry for the science fair?
   A concerned for the students that it might not win
   B confident that it will receive one of the top prizes
   C worried that other schools will come up with better ideas

6 Jamie thinks that it is important to teach science because
   A it gives students skills for their working lives.
   B it provides ongoing opportunities for discovery.
   C it is different to other school subjects.

7 Why does Jamie wish he had discovered a new kind of medicine?
   A He would have enjoyed being recognised for his work.
   B He would have liked to make a difference to people's lives.
   C He would have been happy to pass the information on to students.

12

Vocabulary
research and discovery
▶ CB page 127

1 Match the words (1–8) to their meanings (A–H).

1 records
2 vaccine
3 conclusion
4 experiment
5 process
6 laboratory
7 research
8 discovery

A a place where students learn about science
B a scientific test
C a procedure or method
D work to find out more about a topic
E something which prevents some illnesses
F we keep these to refer to later if necessary
G something you (or others) didn't know before
H something you deduce from certain facts

2 Choose the correct option in italics to complete the sentences.

1 Scientists have recently *made/done* an important discovery about possible life in the solar system.
2 We need to *survey/analyse* these results to see if our ideas were correct or not.
3 Kathy *came/went* up with an excellent idea for our new science project.
4 In the exam, we had to *drive/conduct* an experiment in the laboratory.
5 Did the doctor *take/make* an X-ray of your leg after the accident?
6 I've *got/reached* the conclusion that I am not very good at science!
7 I don't think I've *made/done* enough research to write my assignment yet.
8 They're hoping to *carry/develop* a vaccine that will prevent everyone from getting colds.

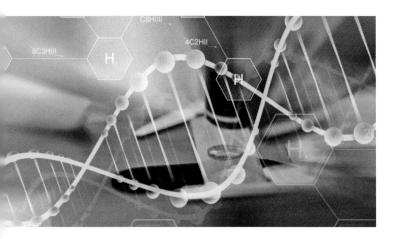

Grammar
reporting verbs ▶ CB page 128

1 Report the statements and questions. Use the reporting verbs in the box.

apologised criticised offered refused
reminded warned

1 'You shouldn't have left work early,' he told me.
He ....
2 'Can I help you carry those boxes?' she asked me.
She ....
3 'No I'm not going to the awards ceremony,' he said.
He ....
4 'Remember to wear your goggles,' our teacher said.
Our teacher ....
5 'Stay away from those chemicals because they're dangerous!' she told us.
She ....
6 'I'm so sorry I missed your concert,' my mum said.
My mum ....

Speaking
Collaborative task and discussion
▶ CB page 129

1 ▶ 24 Read the exam task and the extracts from students' discussions on page 77. Complete the phrases they use to interrupt and encourage their partner with the words in the box. Then listen and check.

about anything don't interrupt isn't
like mean think wanted

Here are some things that people often think about when discussing how important an inventor's job is. Talk to each other about whether inventors do an important job.

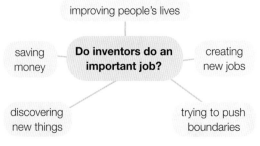

improving people's lives
saving money
Do inventors do an important job?
creating new jobs
discovering new things
trying to push boundaries

Now decide which is the most important aspect of an inventor's job.

Extract A

A: How **(1)** .... saving money? I don't think that's particularly important, to be honest.

B: It depends on the invention. People can use inventions like computers for online shopping, which is cheaper, and that's good for everyone. And what's more, it's cheaper to …

A: I'm sorry to **(2)** .... , but I don't think that's as important as discovering new things.

Extract B

A: How about the idea of pushing boundaries? What do you **(3)** .... about that?

B: I think that's a very important part of an inventor's job, **(4)** .... you?

Extract C

A: … which is why I think discovering new things is vital. An inventor should …

B: Excuse me, I'd just **(5)** .... to say that it's important for inventors to be creative – they have to be free to try different things.

Extract D

A: If inventors create new products, they have to be made or built – and that's how new jobs are created, **(6)** .... it? And also, … Oh sorry, I didn't **(7)** .... to talk for so long! Would you like to add **(8)** .... ?

B: Um, yes, I **(9)** .... to say that having new products to make is also interesting for the people in the workplace.

2 ▶ **25** **Read two of the questions the students were asked after their Part 3 discussion, and the answers they gave. Choose the correct options in italics to complete the answers. Then listen and check.**

A | If you could have invented something in the past, what would it be?

I suppose it **(1)** *relies/depends* on whether I wanted to be remembered for doing something good or making money. If I wanted to do something good, then I'd choose the X-ray machine. On the **(2)** *one/ other* hand, the inventor who came **(3)** *up/out* with hand dryers made lots of money, so I might choose that instead!

B | Some students prefer subjects like music or art to science. Why do you think this is?

I think some students find science difficult because they have to be **(4)** *so/such* accurate. It's easier to talk about , for example, because it's just an opinion, **(5)** *whereas/since* in science you have to be right. **(6)** *Personally/Apparently*, I'd love to be an inventor. It would be very exciting!

Writing

Essay

▶ **CB page 130**

1 **Read the exam task and choose the correct option in italics to complete the essay below.**

In your English class you have recently had a discussion about science in schools. Now your teacher has asked you to write an essay.

Schools should timetable more science lessons. Do you agree?

Notes
Write about
1 interest
2 careers
3 .... (your own idea)

Write an essay using **all** the notes and giving reasons for your point of view. Write **140–190** words.

Should schools timetable more science lessons? **(1)** *While/When* some students who are good at science would be **(2)** *in/on* favour of this, others would disagree. So, who is right?

Unfortunately, some students are just not interested in science. It can be hard, and for that **(3)** *idea/reason*, they are unwilling to try. As a result, **(4)** *however/ whatever* many lessons there were on the timetable, these students would never enjoy them.

(5) *In addition to this/Nevertheless*, science is now an important part of life. **(6)** *If/Unless* students want to have successful careers, then an understanding of science may be necessary. This is a good argument **(7)** *as/in* support of increasing the number of science lessons.

On the other hand, work is not the only thing in life. I **(8)** *think/feel* strongly that there are many other things young people should learn about, such **(9)** *like/as* music and literature. Students should also take part in sport and learn how to keep healthy. Increasing the number of science lessons could take time away from these important subjects.

(10) *For/In* conclusion, I would say that everyone should have a basic understanding of science, but there should be a balance in the school timetable so that students can develop their interest in a wide variety of topics.

2 **Make notes to plan your own answer to the exam task in Activity 1. Then write your answer.**

Useful language

Invitations

1 Match the invitations (1–4) to the responses (A–D).

1 I'm having a birthday party on Saturday. Would you like to come?

2 I'm going shopping later. Do you fancy coming with me?

3 I'm writing to invite you and Tom to our wedding on 8 July. Brian and I do hope you'll be able to come.

4 Jan and I are going to the new restaurant in Bridge Street for a meal on Thursday. Would you like to join us?

A I'd love to. I need to get some new shoes. Where shall we meet?

B Thank you so much for inviting us. We would love to come but unfortunately, we'll be in the USA working for the whole summer.

C Thanks for asking me but I'm afraid I have to work late on Thursday. Have a great time!

D That would be great. Is it at your house? What time do you want people to arrive?

2 Find phrases in Activity 1 used for

    A inviting.   **B** accepting.   **C** thanking.   **D** refusing.

3 Which invitation in Activity 1 is the most formal?

Opinions and agreement/disagreement

1 Match the sentences (1–10) to the situations (A–F). Some sentences match more than one situation.

1 I feel very strongly that students shouldn't have to pay for public transport.

2 I like this book, don't you?

3 I see what you mean, but I'm not too sure I agree.

4 Yes, I'm with you – up to a point.

5 So, what do you think about the new reality show?

6 I completely agree. The film was so boring.

7 In my opinion, the test was really hard! What did you think?

8 You're right. I totally agree.

9 I don't think it was a good match. How did you feel about it?

10 No, I don't think so.

A asking for an opinion

B asking for agreement

C giving an opinion

D expressing agreement

E expressing partial agreement

F expressing disagreement

Suggestions, recommendations and advice

1 **Complete the dialogues with the correct form of the verbs in brackets.**

1 **A:** I'm having real problems deciding what to study at university. What would you advise me _____ (*do*)?

B: If I were you, I'd _____ (*talk*) to the career's advisor at school. She's really good.

2 **A:** I've got some visitors from Norway over for the weekend. Where do you recommend _____ (*go*) for a meal?

B: I can thoroughly _____ (*recommend*) the New Park Hotel. They serve some lovely traditional English food.

3 **A:** OK. So, we're doing this project about fashion together. Where do you suggest we _____ (*start*)?

B: Why don't we _____ (*do*) some research online about fashion trends? Then we can _____ (*download*) some useful information.

4 **A:** I've had a terrible headache all day. What should I _____ (*do*) about it?

B: I think you should _____ (*get*) some sleep. You look really tired.

5 **A:** I'm staying in London for a few days. Any ideas about places _____ (*visit*)?

B: How about _____ (*go*) to an art exhibition at the National Gallery? There's usually something good on there. Or you could always _____ (*go*) to one of the musicals in the West End.

6 **A:** We could _____ (*get*) a good DVD to watch this weekend. Any suggestions?

B: Yes. Let's _____ (*get*) *Rules Not to Follow*. We haven't seen that yet.

Requests, offers and permission

1 **Match the speakers (1–8) to the dialogues on the right (A–H).**

1 two sales assistants

2 a customer and a waiter

3 two strangers in the street

4 two teachers

5 a candidate for a job and an employer

6 a boy and his father

7 two school friends

8 a supermarket assistant and a customer

A **A:** <u>Could you</u> get me some water, please?

B: <u>Certainly</u>. I'll bring some immediately.

B **A:** <u>I wonder if you could</u> help me. I'm looking for Trent Road.

B: <u>Sure</u>. Turn left just after the church.

C **A:** Could I have a quick word? <u>Would you mind</u> checking this student's essay for me?

B: <u>No problem</u>.

D **A:** <u>I'll deal with</u> this next customer if you like.

B: I'm not too busy now, so <u>it's OK. Thanks anyway</u>.

E **A:** Sue, <u>can I</u> use your mobile for a moment? I left mine at home.

B: <u>That's fine</u>. Here you are.

F **A:** <u>Would you like me to</u> carry that shopping to the car for you?

B: <u>That's very kind of you</u>.

G **A:** <u>Is it OK if I</u> borrow the car tonight to go to Mack's party?

B: <u>Sorry</u>, not tonight. I'll be using it myself.

H **A:** <u>Could you please</u> let me know about the job as soon as possible?

B: <u>Of course</u>. We'll contact you next week.

2 **Put the underlined phrases in Activity 1 under the correct heading.**

Requesting

Can you … ?

_____

_____

_____

Responding to requests

I'm afraid I can't …

_____

_____

_____

Offering

Shall I … ?

_____

Responding to offers

Thanks. That's brilliant.

_____

Asking for permission

May I … ?

_____

Giving/Refusing permission

Yes, of course you may/can.

_____

Useful phrases: Speaking

1 Match the headings in the box to the groups of phrases (1–8).

Adding
Asking for repetition or clarification
Clarifying
Giving yourself time to think
Interrupting   Involving your partner
Organising the discussion
Speculating

---

1 ....

Could you repeat that, please?
What exactly do you mean?
Are you saying that … ?

2 ....

What I mean is …
What I'm trying to say is…

3 ....

Could I just say here that …
Excuse me, but I think …
Sorry to interrupt, but …

4 ....

As well as that, I think that …
I'd like to add that …

5 ....

Let me think.
I haven't thought about that before.
That's an interesting question.

6 ....

Let's start by thinking about …
Shall we start with … ?
Shall we move on to … ?
We haven't discussed …, have we?
It's time we made a decision.

7 ....

So, what do you think?
Do you agree?
How do you feel about … ?
Have you got any experience of … ?

8 ....

I imagine that …
It looks as though …
It seems to me that …
It might …

Useful phrases: Writing

1 Choose the phrase (A, B or C) which is the most formal in each situation.

1 Addressing a person in a letter or email
  A Dear Katy,
  B Hi Pam,
  C Dear Sir,

2 Signing off a letter or email
  A Love, Pete
  B Best wishes, Mary
  C Yours sincerely, Eve Bower

3 Starting a letter or email
  A Great to hear from you.
  B It was kind of you to contact me.
  C Thanks for your letter/email.

4 Giving a reason for writing
  A I am writing to apply for the job advertised in the newspaper.
  B I'm writing to let you know I'll be back in London next month.
  C I'm writing to say thanks for such a lovely birthday present.

5 Referring to a previous letter/email
  A I'm so happy to hear your news.
  B With reference to your previous letter, I …
  C You sounded a bit worried in your last email.

6 Closing a letter or email
  A Please write soon.
  B I hope to hear from you soon.
  C I look forward to hearing from you.

2 Choose the type of writing task where you are most likely to find the phrases.

1	On the other hand,	*essay/email*
2	How would you feel if …?	*article/report*
3	It's one of the best films I've seen.	*review/report*
4	It is widely believed that …	*email/essay*
5	It is based on a true story.	*review/essay*
6	It's definitely worth reading.	*review/report*
7	I would recommend making changes to …	*essay/report*
8	Many people go on holiday, but do they enjoy it?	*report/article*
9	The plot is extremely exciting.	*essay/review*
10	On balance, I believe that more people spend …	*essay/email*

Practice test

Reading and Use of English

Part 1

For questions **1–8**, read the text below and decide which answer (**A**, **B**, **C** or **D**) best fits each gap. There is an example at the beginning (**0**).

Example

0 **A** requirement   **B** <u>necessity</u>   **C** want   **D** desire

---

How to invent things

Inventions are created through **(0)** ...., and this is the best **(1)** .... of creating something. The first step is identifying a need – either someone **(2)** .... there is a lack of something useful or they decide life would be easier if only there was a device that would do a task more quickly. This is when creative people get **(3)** .... and make the gadget for themselves. Another way to invent something is by observing someone **(4)** .... to do something and concluding that there must be a better way to get the **(5)** .... done. This can occur by **(6)** .... – you see someone slip on the ice and invent a new kind of snowshoe – or it can be deliberate. Perhaps you want to start up a business but you don't know what kind of product to **(7)** .... on. So, you look for ideas. You see someone battling with a **(8)** .... and come up with a solution – and bingo! Your invention is born.

1	**A** power	**B** method	**C** habit	**D** force
2	**A** realises	**B** recammends	**C** tells	**D** values
3	**A** busy	**B** alive	**C** keen	**D** fast
4	**A** arguing	**B** struggling	**C** concentrating	**D** competing
5	**A** exercise	**B** subject	**C** task	**D** question
6	**A** incident	**B** accident	**C** example	**D** instance
7	**A** plan	**B** attempt	**C** direct	**D** focus
8	**A** problem	**B** matter	**C** trouble	**D** factor

Part 2

For questions **9–16**, read the text below and think of the word which best fits each gap. Use only one word in each gap. There is an example at the beginning (**0**).

Example

0	been

Does the weather change how we feel?

For decades, researchers have **(0)** .... trying to establish whether there is a relationship between the weather and mood. While some say the weather has only a small effect on mood, others claim that weather conditions **(9)** .... as humidity, sunshine and temperature can affect us significantly. **(10)** .... to these studies, we become sleepy in humid conditions. This makes it harder **(11)** .... us to concentrate. However, sunshine produces a natural feel-good chemical that makes us feel awake and happy. **(12)** .... also seems that higher temperatures reduce feelings of anxiety, so, unsurprisingly, the more sunshine hours we experience, the more optimistic we feel.

Psychologists, **(13)** .... course, believe it's up to us to create **(14)** .... own positive experiences, whatever the weather. For example, when the rain **(15)** .... falling, we should listen to music, read a book or do some exercise. When there's sunshine, we should take advantage of the light, **(16)** .... increases our serotonin levels. Whatever the science says, I know that I just enjoy the sunshine!

Part 3

For questions **17–24**, read the text below. Use the word given in capitals at the end of some of the lines to form a word that fits in the gap **in the same line**. There is an example at the beginning (**0**).

Example

0	stressful

Holidays: delight or disappointment?

Going on holiday can be **(0)** .... and it often starts before you even leave home. The list of things to do seems **(17)** .... and it isn't too long before your **(18)** .... starts to run out. Eventually, however, your bags are packed and you're setting off for some rest and **(19)** ....

After a tiring journey, you **(20)** .... arrive at your resort, only to find the hotel is still being built, the air-conditioning is broken and it's incredibly **(21)** .... everywhere. There's no evening entertainment and even the sightseeing is **(22)** .... , with nothing special to see. Then there's the long journey home, when the flight's delayed and you arrive home exhausted.

If this is what always happens, why do we put ourselves through it? I guess we always hope there will be an **(23)** .... next year. After all, it's thrilling to visit different places and have new and **(24)** .... experiences and not every holiday turns out to be a disappointment!

STRESS
END
PATIENT
RELAX
FINAL
NOISE
EXCITE

IMPROVE
PREDICT

Part 4

For questions **25–30**, complete the second sentence so that it has a similar meaning to the first sentence, using the word given. **Do not change the word given.** You must use between two and five words, including the word given.

Here is an example (**0**).

Example

0   'I'm really sorry that I broke your new phone,' Belle said.

      APOLOGISED

      Belle .... my new phone.

The gap can be filled by the words 'apologised for breaking', so you write:

Example

0	apologised for breaking

---

25   'I don't like this pizza,' said Vicky.

      KEEN

      Vicky said she .... the pizza.

26   Michael can't swim very well.

      AT

      Michael .... swimming.

27   Karl made me jump when he suddenly walked into the room.

      TOOK

      Karl .... when he suddenly walked into the room.

28   They're building a new sports centre in the town.

      BUILT

      A new sports centre .... in the town.

29   The entry ticket to the theme park includes one free ride.

      IS

      One free ride .... the entry ticket to the theme park.

30   'Remember to lock the door when you leave,' Mum told me.

      REMINDED

      Mum .... the door when I left.

Part 5

You are going to read a newspaper article about a festival which takes place each winter in Venice, Italy. For questions **31–36**, choose the answer (**A**, **B**, **C** or **D**) which you think fits best according to the text.

Venetian Masquerade

Last month Liz Ford put on a mask and set off for Carnevale, Venice's popular mid-winter festival.

At carnival time in Italy's watery city, wearing a mask appears to be a compulsory part of the uniform. So, when I attended the carnival last month with my friend Asha we decided it was something that we too had to put on. We browsed the stalls lining the streets selling what has become the symbol of the carnival. But as there were literally hundreds to choose from, it didn't make for an easy decision and I wasn't satisfied until I had finally settled on one with a few decorative feathers and was ready to take part in the festivities.

The people of Venice have been celebrating Carnevale since the fifteenth century. In those days, parties were arranged where rich and poor alike hid their identity behind masks and danced the nights away to forget the difficulties of winter. The tradition gradually faded away until, in 1979, it was brought back to life, becoming one of the world's most popular festivals. Today, however, some of the city's residents complain that the carnival is nothing compared to its former self, and is purely geared towards bringing in money.

The festivities begin with La Festa delle Marie, a parade through the city and a taste of what is to come. Throughout the following days, guests attend fabulous masked balls, where they mingle with others, watch acrobats and artists and dine on
line 29 delightful food and drink – the carnival is truly a feast for the senses. The highlight of the festival is, without doubt, the Grand Masked Ball, located in a beautiful palace and a chance to show off your knowledge of Venetian traditions, such as performing the steps of the ancient quadrilles dances. That won't be me, then!

Asha and I spent our days in Venice exploring the narrow waterways, hidden shops and cafés. The bustling crowds and party atmosphere were electrifying but, without doubt, the highlight of our trip was dressing for a special dinner on our final night. We put on our masks, hired dresses and no longer felt out of place with the other party-goers. We boarded the boat at St Mark's bay, lit by street lamps. As the gondola swept up canals past ancient buildings in the shadows of night, I noticed an air of mystery that hadn't been revealed during daylight. Somebody on board passed around sparklers and we waved the fiery sticks at onlookers as we passed under bridges. Putting on a mask makes you an instant hit at carnival time.

Leaving the boat in San Polo, we headed for dinner. Walking into the candle-lit restaurant was like stepping back in time. More than fifty people were already seated, every face hidden behind a mask, just as they would have been centuries ago. At first I found it difficult talking to people I couldn't see properly, though I soon started enjoying myself. The entertainment, provided by modern dancers, wasn't quite of the era the feast was meant to represent. But the food was superb and the setting magnificent.

After our meal, Asha and I went out into the busy streets again and found our way to a jazz bar which, though it played more popular music than jazz, was the ideal place to finish off our stay in Venice. As dawn broke, the party carried on, but we sadly made our way towards the vaporetto, the Venetian waterbus which carried us along the canals towards the airport for our morning flight back to London. We finally took off our masks. The party was over for me and Asha, but I hope we'll be back again one day.

31 When talking about carnival masks, the writer says that she

    A was careful about her choice.

    B was amazed by the number of stalls selling them.

    C was originally unenthusiastic about wearing one.

    D was determined to look different from everyone else.

32 According to the writer, some people feel that today's Carnevale

    A takes people's attention away from bad weather.

    B doesn't deserve its international reputation.

    C is simply a money-making scheme.

    D is more interesting than it used to be.

33 What does *a feast for the senses* mean in line 29?

    A something that is delicious to eat

    B something that is pleasing to experience

    C something that is unexpected

    D something that provides a chance to meet people

34 As the writer went out on the final evening of her stay, she

    A was pleased to be wearing a suitable costume.

    B was embarrassed by the attention she received from spectators.

    C was impressed with the way the streets had been decorated.

    D was surprised that the city looked so strange at night.

35 What comment does the writer make about the dinner she attended?

    A The food was disappointing.

    B The location was too dark.

    C The customers were unfriendly.

    D The entertainment was unsuitable.

36 In the final paragraph, the writer

    A feels confident that she will be back in Venice in the near future.

    B is unimpressed with the transport which she has to use.

    C is disappointed with the way the last evening finishes.

    D expresses regret at having to leave the party.

Part 6

You are going to read a newspaper article about climbing Everest. Six sentences have been removed from the article. Choose from the sentences (**A–G**) the one which fits each gap (**37–42**). There is one extra sentence which you do not need to use.

Climbing Everest

Mountaineer and author Andy Cave explains its beautiful, fatal attraction.

It hurts. Anybody who climbs above 8,000 m without oxygen and says it doesn't is a liar. I take six steps and then bend over my ice axe, resting my head in the snow. Babu Chiri Sherpa and my fellow-climber David are doing exactly the same. A few minutes later, we are standing on the very top of Shishapangma (8,027 m), exhausted but very happy. The white mountains of the Himalaya run off to the curved horizon, dividing the green hills of Nepal and the endless desert of Tibet. You can see the giant, Everest, to the east.

Why does Everest continue to attract people? Although the media seem obsessed with the risk and loss associated with mountain climbing, clearly, this is not what motivates mountaineers themselves. Look at portraits of climbers returning from the summit of Everest; look at the triumph on their faces. Yes, they also look tired. **37** More than anyone, they understand the risks involved and they look relieved to be back on firm ground.

The truth is that the thought of standing on the highest point of the earth (8,848 m) is a dream for many climbers. And not just a dream. Today, with a modest technical ability, climbing the mountain is achievable. Last year alone over 600 people reached the summit, some of them with little mountaineering experience.

In recent years, for various reasons, the chances of climbing the peak successfully have improved considerably. There are several reasons for this. **38** As well as this, the clothing available for today's mountaineers is made with sophisticated designs and hi-tech fabrics and the weight of equipment such as crampons and karabiners has been dramatically reduced.

To climb on Everest is to walk through history, myth and legend. The achievement of Hillary, Tenzing and team making the first ascent in 1953 is well-known to all of us, but the real romance and mystery is reserved for the story of George Mallory and Andrew Irvine in 1924. The two men were attempting Everest from Tibet via the North Col. **39**

Every climber has a view on the fate of Mallory and Irvine, on whether or not they reached the summit. In 1999, American alpinist Conrad Anker found Mallory's body on the north side of Everest, but without his camera. **40** His partner Irvine's body has never been recovered.

The normal route up Everest, via the South Col, is not a technically difficult climb by today's standards, but it still commands respect. In 1996, a single storm killed eight people and it made no difference whether they were inexperienced mountaineers or sherpas. Mountaineers have to accept the risks involved and put in place strategies to reduce them. **41**

For many, climbing Everest will be considered pointless, but its attraction will never die. Perhaps the desire to climb so high is part of the human desire to explore and to push the boundaries. To climb any mountain is to take a risk. **42** Perhaps George Mallory understood the motivation of most climbers when he wrote, 'What we get from this adventure is sheer joy. And joy is, after all, the end of life. We do not live to eat and make money.'

A   This is unfortunate as scientists believe that the film could have been developed, which might have solved the mystery.

B   And if human beings had never taken any and always played safe, we'd all be sitting in caves, living like animals.

C   The last known sighting of them was on 8 June of that year, through a gap in the clouds, just a few hundred metres from the summit.

D   However, there is also a longing to enjoy the moment before returning to routine daily life.

E   Good ones go bravely into the mountains, not blindly.

F   The combination of sun, wind and cold has roughened their skin and they will be dehydrated.

G   One is that, above 8,000 m on Everest, almost everyone breathes bottled oxygen and the bottles used now are much lighter than their predecessors.

Part 7

You are going to an article about coping with stress. For questions **43–52**, choose from the sections (**A–D**). The sections may be chosen more than once.

Which section

advises against a modern way of doing something?	43
says we should imagine a different outcome to a situation?	44
talks about fear of the unknown?	45
tells us that we can learn from the past?	46
approves of both a modern and an outdated way of doing the same thing?	47
focuses on the importance of establishing a routine?	48
suggests following another person's example?	49
encourages us to plan ahead?	50
gives specific examples of difficult situations in the past?	51
mentions an activity that has more than one positive effect on us?	52

Coping with life's stresses

A Running

Most of us are aware of the physical benefits of running, but equally important for our well-being are the mental effects: increased clarity of thought, stress relief, etc. When we are running, endorphins are released which give our spirits a definite lift and send the blood to the brain, which makes it easier to think clearly. Is there a good way to run though? An excellent tip is to watch an eight-year-old girl running. Just running robotically on a machine with music blasting through our earphones, as so many of us do today, is not going to get those happy hormones buzzing. Learn from the child – the steps are springy, the foot gets off the floor quickly and comes down lightly. Tune in to your feet and not your music player.

B Sleeping

Concern about how much sleep we get and worry about all the things we have to do can only increase our problems. If you are a worrier, you will worry – and this affects your sleep. And we all know that a foggy, sleep-deprived brain can't work well. So, stick to the ground rules: go to bed and get up at the same time every day, and allow some time to wind down before bed. As for your worries, assign yourself a 'worry period'. This should be in the same place, at the same time every day. Give yourself 15–20 minutes to write down and contemplate a to-do list – it can really help to look at the things you need to get through the next day. And if you're worrying about worrying keeping you awake, remind yourself that your body actually needs less sleep than you think. Although we're told to get eight hours, six to seven hours is absolutely fine.

C Dealing with change

Most of us, when faced with change, instinctively react by wanting to hold onto things as they are. But you're better at coping with change than you think. In fact, you will already have coped with lots of it in your life and have masses of experience to draw on. So, next time you're faced with a change that feels terrifying, do this: write down all the changes you have experienced at different times in your life. Perhaps you once had to change school, had a new baby in the family or moved home and so on. Underneath, write down the coping strategies you had to learn in each of these change situations. The point is that those valuable life skills helped you once and will do so again if you can just remember them and remove some of the inevitable fear that accompanies change.

D Putting it on paper

Sometimes we get stressed about things that have happened and we just think about them over and over again. 'What if I'd said … ?' 'Why didn't he … ?' Writing down the things that are worrying us or have made us angry can be very therapeutic. It is a way of setting a thought free. Once it's on the page, or screen, we can read it, reread it, delete it or reflect upon it. Writing allows us to access the logical and creative parts of the brain as we connect meaning together. Try it: take something that has bothered you – this could be a conversation or argument which didn't turn out the way you wanted – and write what you wish you'd said or the words of sympathy you wish you'd been offered. Writing a blog may have overtaken diaries, but they are both a means of presenting your thoughts. The style doesn't need to be of a prize-winning standard to have value! It's also something you can look back on in years to come.

Writing

Part 1

You must answer this question. Write your answer in **140–190** words in an appropriate style.

In your English class you have been talking about whether life is better now than it was before because of the internet. Now your English teacher has asked you to write an essay.

Write an essay using **all** the notes and give reasons for your point of view.

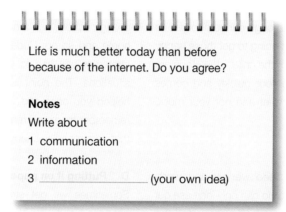

Life is much better today than before because of the internet. Do you agree?

Notes

Write about

1 communication

2 information

3 _____ (your own idea)

Part 2

Write an answer to one of the questions **2–4** in this part. Write your answer in **140–190** words in an appropriate style.

2   You have received this email from your Australian friend, Kate.

> Hi!
>
> I'll be coming back specially for our class reunion! I know its Clare's birthday too but I've no idea what to get her as a present. Can you give me some ideas? I'll be in town for a few days after the reunion. What do you recommend to do nearby? It's been years since my last visit – so I'll need ideas!
>
> Looking forward to seeing you there,
>
> Kate

Write your **email**.

3   You see this advert in an international film magazine.

Film reviews wanted!

We are looking for reviews of a film you think should be included in our list of the best films of the last year. Your review should include details of the film, what you liked about it and why you think it should be included in our list. Would you recommend it to other people your age?

The best reviews will be published in our magazine at the end of the year.

Write your **review**.

4   You see this announcement on your college noticeboard.

> Do you have a favourite spot where you like to chill out? Maybe you read there or listen to music. We are looking for articles with the title *My favourite spot* to include in the college magazine. Tell us why this place is so important to you, what you like to do there and how you discovered it.

Write your **article**.

Listening

Part 1 26

You will hear people talking in eight different situations. For questions **1–8**, choose the best answer (**A**, **B** or **C**).

1   You hear a boy talking about a recent flight he has been on. What spoiled the experience for him?
   A his fear of the take-off
   B the length of the journey
   C a delay caused by the weather

2   You hear a woman leaving a voicemail message. What does she want to do?
   A rearrange a meeting
   B explain why she missed a meeting
   C get help preparing for a meeting

3   You hear an actress giving an interview about a recent performance. Why did she take the role?
   A She thought it was an exciting challenge.
   B She hadn't done a Shakespeare play before.
   C She wanted to work with a particular director.

4   You hear a swimmer talking about a recent race. Why did he make a false start?
   A He was badly prepared.
   B He was misled.
   C He was nervous.

5   You hear two friends talking about the sales. What advice does the girl give the boy?
   A not to go by car
   B not to get there too early
   C not to expect good bargains

6   You hear two friends talking about a recent TV programme. What did they both dislike about it?
   A It was too old-fashioned.
   B It wasn't true to the book.
   C The main actor wasn't right for the part.

7   You hear part of a radio news programme. What does the presenter say about the severe weather?
   A It caused short interruptions in power supply.
   B It came as a surprise to many people.
   C It is expected to continue.

8   You hear two friends talking about a new laptop. What is the boy unhappy with?
   A the after-sales service
   B the start-up speed
   C the size and weight

Part 2 27

You will hear a girl called Samantha talking to her class about a wedding she attended. For questions **9–18**, complete the sentences with a word or short phrase.

A wedding in Paris

Samantha says her **(9)** .... was unable to attend the wedding in Paris.

Samantha was upset that the hotel didn't have a **(10)** ....

Samantha was annoyed that she'd forgotten to pack the **(11)** .... she wanted to.

The **(12)** .... in the town hall particularly impressed Samantha.

Samantha liked the fact that a **(13)** .... took pictures of the bride and groom.

The city tour was exciting for Samantha because of her interest in **(14)** ....

Samantha uses the word **(15)** .... to describe the setting for the wedding reception.

Samantha ate a specially prepared **(16)** .... meal at the wedding.

Samantha was surprised that there were no **(17)** .... at the wedding.

The DJ played a song called **(18)** .... , which Samantha liked very much.

Part 3 28

You will hear five short extracts in which women are talking about writers they like. For questions **19–23**, choose from the list (**A–H**) what made each speaker start reading the writer's books. There are three extra letters which you do not need to use.

A	a film adaptation of one of the books	Speaker 1 **19**
B	an educational requirement	Speaker 2 **20**
C	a personal recommendation	Speaker 3 **21**
D	a desire to be up-to-date with modern writers	Speaker 4 **22**
E	a doctor's advice	Speaker 5 **23**
F	a coincidence	
G	a combination of factors	
H	a TV review	

Part 4 29

You will hear an interview with a woman called Vicky Baines, who teaches a type of exercise called Zumba. For questions **24–30**, choose the best answer (**A**, **B** or **C**).

24 Vicky decided to become a Zumba instructor when she

   A   was praised for her technique.

   B   attended a session with a friend.

   C   became unemployed.

25 What does Vicky say when asked about the popularity of Zumba?

   A   She is surprised that so many people are interested in it.

   B   She wondered whether people would take it seriously as a way to keep fit.

   C   She thinks people have become bored with other types of exercise.

26 Vicky thinks that people enjoy Zumba because

   A   it doesn't require much effort to get right.

   B   it's a good way to meet other people.

   C   it can be done individually at home.

27 Vicky thinks that to become good at Zumba, you need

   A   a basic sense of rhythm.

   B   a talent for learning different steps.

   C   a certain amount of flexibility.

28 What does Vicky enjoy so much about teaching Zumba?

   A   choosing the music she plays while the class works out

   B   inventing unusual routines for her class to try out

   C   seeing people become more energetic

29 What does Vicky identify as an unexpected benefit of doing Zumba?

   A   It makes the body stronger.

   B   It increases coordination for everyday tasks.

   C   It makes people feel happier.

30 What is Vicky going to do next?

   A   film an exercise video

   B   teach a new form of Zumba

   C   start up a children's class

Speaking

Part 1

The interlocutor will ask you and the other candidate some questions about yourselves.

▶ 30 Listen to the recording and answer the questions. Pause the recording after each bleep and give your answer.

Part 2

The interlocutor will ask you and the other candidate to talk on your own about some photographs.

▶ 31 Listen to the recording and answer the questions. When you hear two bleeps, answer the question. You have one minute. When you hear one bleep, answer the second question. You have thirty seconds.

Candidate A

Why have the people chosen to stay in these places?

Candidate B

What are the people enjoying about these activities?

Part 3

The interlocutor will ask you and the other candidate to discuss something together.

▶ 32 Look at the task and listen to the interlocutor's instructions. When you hear the bleep, discuss the task. You have two minutes.

shopping online

playing computer games

Does technology always make people's lives better?

using social networking sites

saving or wasting time

Listen to the interlocutor's instructions. When you hear the bleep, discuss and make your decision. You have one minute.

Part 4

The interlocutor will ask you and the other candidate questions related to the topic of Part 3.

▶ 33 Listen to the recording and answer the interlocutor's questions. Pause the recording when you hear each bleep and discuss the question with the other candidate.

Audio scripts

Unit 1, Listening Activity 1

Track 01

N = Narrator   S = Speaker

1

N: You hear a man talking about a friend who lost her job.

S1: Like most other people I know, I use social networking sites a lot. It's great to post photos and look at other people's to see what they've been doing. I've got loads of friends and I can keep in touch with everyone. But you have to be careful. A friend of mine had a really bad experience. She took some time off work to go skiing but she told her boss she was ill. You can guess what happened … She posted photos of herself in Switzerland and someone told her boss. She's looking for another job now!

2

N: You hear a girl talking about a time she used her mobile phone on public transport.

S2: I'm never without my mobile phone and I have a fear of losing it. I use it at home, at school, in the street – I hate being out of touch with my friends. But I've stopped using it on trains. Last month my mother phoned me while I was on the train. We often used to chat during the journey, but this time was different: she was telling me off about my recent homework grades, and everyone on the train overheard our conversation. It all went very quiet. I was so embarrassed!

3

N: You hear a boy talking about a postcard he sent to a friend.

S3: Like most people these days, I rarely write letters to friends –I usually email or text. But I quite like sending a postcard if I'm on holiday. It's sort of traditional and personal, and it's nice for a friend to get the picture, isn't it? Well, last year I sent my friend a postcard from Mexico. It was a stunning picture of a long sandy beach. But – you won't believe this – it was eighteen months before it was delivered to my friend! I have no idea what happened – it probably went around the world several times before my friend got it! She thought it was funny, though I was a bit cross.

4

N: You hear a woman talking about sending an email.

S4: It's so easy to email friends – one minute on your computer or phone, press a key, and you've done it. But the problem is it's very easy to make a mistake. We've all done it: written a long email and then pressed the wrong key, and it disappears. I made a really big mistake last month. I had an argument with my best friend, Eva. It was about something very silly, but I was feeling angry, so I wrote an email to another friend telling him all about it; I said some bad things about Eva. Well, the moment I sent the email, I realised I'd clicked the wrong button and sent it to everyone in my address book, including Eva! She isn't my best friend anymore!

Unit 2, Speaking Activity 1

Track 02

Your photos show people who are wearing special clothes in different situations. I'd like you to compare the photos and say why the people have decided to wear special clothes in these situations.

Unit 2, Speaking Activity 2

Track 03

Both pictures show people who are wearing special clothes, but they're in different situations. In the first picture the skier is spending her free time enjoying herself, whereas in the second one the people are obviously working in a kitchen. This means they have different reasons for the clothes they've decided to wear. I think the skier is a girl. She needs to have clothes that will protect her against the cold weather on the mountain, so she is wearing thick clothes. She probably chose them herself because she wants to look good when she's skiing. She's also wearing a helmet, in case she falls and hurts herself.

The people in the second picture, however, probably didn't choose their clothes themselves – they have to wear them because their clothes are important for the job they're doing. I think they're baking a cake and they have to cover their hair and their ordinary clothes so that the food they're cooking stays safe and clean. The clothes are also special for chefs so that other people can identify them. They all look very interested in their work.

Unit 2, Listening Activity 2

Track 04

Winning the lottery has completely transformed my life! I used to ignore all the advertising campaigns for the lottery because I didn't think I would ever win. But one day, I did some shopping at the supermarket and then at the grocer's in town, and on my way back home, I walked past a bookshop near my house. They had a sign outside about lottery tickets, so I decided to give it a go.

However, I forgot all about it until I heard no one had claimed the week's prize. I found the ticket in my bag and checked it. I couldn't believe it when I saw I had all the winning numbers! I was so surprised! But after the initial shock, I actually felt worried. I had no idea what I should do with one million pounds!

You might think this was strange but whereas most people might go out and buy a big house and a fancy car, I got myself a watch because my old one was broken. It wasn't particularly expensive – it just seemed wrong to go out and buy stuff I didn't need.

Then I realised I could help other people and I looked for things to do in my town. I made a donation towards a machine that the hospital needed. I also helped the school I went to when I was young by giving them the money to build a library. That's the thing I feel most proud of. Education's so important.

I helped my family too, of course. My parents needed a new kitchen, so I paid for that work to be done, and I bought my brother a camera, which he was really pleased with because he uses it for his job.

I've also had the opportunity to travel abroad for the first time – with my best friend. She suggested Milan, Italy, but in the end we decided to go to Spain – I've always wanted to go. Now I'm planning to visit Japan. Yes, I've been very lucky!

Unit 3, Listening Activities 1 and 2

Track 05

1 All types of cookery have become popular recently and that's mainly down to the number of famous chefs on TV. I run a cookery course at the centre and in recent months I've had to start another class too because it's become so popular! I don't teach everything about cooking, obviously – my course is all about baking – making cakes and biscuits and yummy things like that with loads of calories! You might think that the people who come to my courses are all mums and grannies but you'd be surprised to see the number of teenage boys I have in the class at the moment! They're very good too.

2 When you watch those chefs on TV, you would imagine you need to be fairly rich. The items they use to cook that lovely food are very expensive. My class is all about teaching people how to cook really well with very little money. It's amazing how easy it is. When I started the course, I was happy to get five or six students but now the class is full and I have a waiting list. I'm glad it's so popular. I feel as though I'm really helping people at a time when they have to save as much money as they can, and that's great.

3 Good food is a real pleasure. Most of us enjoy going out for a nice meal. However, these days we also know how dangerous it can be. Putting on weight is a problem. My cookery course tries to help people who have problems with their weight and also their families. I do not run a dieting club! I teach people about food and what it does for our bodies. My students learn how to plan and cook well-balanced meals so that they eat everything they need to be healthy. They lose weight but they also learn eating habits that will help them stay slim.

4 My cookery course is aimed at people who want to cook food that is a bit special – not your normal meat and vegetable dishes! I know many students come to the course because they have a real passion for cooking. The TV cooking competitions are to thank for this! People see others just like them cooking amazing meals and think, 'Why not me?' So, I show them how. A couple of my ex-students have actually gone on TV competitions since I taught them and one girl – only eighteen – won a major prize. I was very proud!

Unit 4, Speaking Activity 1

Track 06

Your photos show people travelling in different ways. I'd like you to compare the photos and say how you think the people are feeling.

Unit 4, Speaking Activity 2

Track 07

1 Do you enjoy travelling on the underground?

2 Do you enjoy travelling by plane?

3 Do you think it's worse to be delayed at a train station or an airport? Why?

Unit 4, Listening Activities 1 and 2

Track 08

Hi, everyone. I'm Jack, and I'm going to tell you about my recent trip to the Arctic.

I've always been curious about cold places, and it was a long-held ambition of mine to be able to visit the Arctic Circle in winter. I wanted to have a *real* adventure, so I decided to go backpacking there with a few friends. Even though we weren't going to the North Pole, it was still a rather unusual thing for young people to do. Some of my friends thought it would be a bit difficult and even frightening, but I thought it was challenging and couldn't wait to go.

We arrived inside the Arctic Circle by plane and set off by bus to explore the countryside. We couldn't afford hotels, so we had planned to stay in family homes. However, the hostels were excellent – very comfortable and welcoming – so we decided to stay in those.

I had done lots of research about life in the Arctic and so I knew it would be cold and snowy, but the wind was totally unexpected. It was so strong that it meant temperatures felt even colder than they actually were – and they were around minus ten! We had to buy extra hats, gloves and boots to keep us warm. I was glad that I'd brought several scarves with me as they sometimes got wet in the snow.

We had made plans to visit a husky farm – they're the working dogs that pull sledges across the snow in remote places. The farm we visited had around eighty dogs, all being trained for their working lives. I talked to some of the trainers there, and one of the things they said was that female dogs make the best leaders, which I found surprising. Apparently, although all the dogs are obviously strong – I suppose they have to be because of the work they do – females are considered to be more intelligent. I also didn't know that teams of huskies take part in races too, and once I found out, I was sorry there weren't any of those when we were there. They would have been fun to see.

One more reason I'd wanted to go to the Arctic in winter was because I wanted the chance to see the Northern Lights. These appear as green or yellow lights in the night sky, and they're caused by sun particles falling into the earth's atmosphere. Unfortunately, they're only visible if the weather is clear and frosty rather than cloudy, so lots of people who travel to the Arctic just to see them are disappointed. The lights can be seen from October to March, although February is considered to be the best month to catch them. We camped out a long way from the pollution caused by the town lights because we thought that would give us the best chance to see them. After several hours of waiting in the cold, suddenly, there they were! And I'd say they were worth waiting for – they were spectacular! They looked just like smoke – and they were slightly scary too!

My Arctic adventure was only short, but it was memorable and I can't wait to go back. Next time I'll go in the summer though, so I can experience the midnight sun. It'll be a different kind of adventure, but I'm sure it will be equally enjoyable. You'd all love it, I'm sure!

Unit 5, Listening Activities 1 and 2

Track 09

1   I hate shopping – there are always so many people and it's always a struggle to get what you want. I often come home with something I don't like and I spend too much on my credit card. Last week I went to buy a birthday present for my cousin and it was a nightmare! The girl in the shop couldn't have been kinder, but even so, it was impossible to identify anything that was suitable for a present. In the end, I decided to get my cousin an online voucher so that she could buy something for herself.

2   I usually go shopping with my friends at the weekend, and we spend ages in the shopping centre. We enjoy spending time in a café and going to the cinema as well as shopping – we always have a great time. This time, though, things went wrong. I was looking for a special present for my best friend. The centre was so full it was difficult to walk around, but worse was the fact that we'd spent too long in the cinema and I had to find something before the shop closed. I managed it, but I'm not very happy with my choice.

3   My family all enjoy shopping, but I feel it's a waste of time. I have better things to do! But if I need to buy someone a present, then I have to do it. Last weekend I was in that situation, and I'd left it very late to buy this present for my sister. I looked everywhere, then decided that I'd buy a book but I needed advice. The man in the shop wasn't interested in my problems and in the end, I found something myself. I was able to pay by credit card, which was convenient, but I wasn't happy with his manner.

4   I actually usually like shopping – it's always interesting wandering around looking at new products and seeing what is fashionable. Last weekend it was horrible, though. One of my favourite shops was giving special discounts and so it was packed with people. I had wanted to buy myself something with some birthday money I'd been given, but by the time I'd waited ages just to get into the shop, I'd lost interest. I might do my shopping online in future – I can do that whenever I want at home!

Unit 5, Speaking Activity 3

Track 10

A: So, let's think about advertisements influencing children. What do you think? Is advertising a bad thing for them?

B: To be honest, I don't think children really watch them – they probably ignore them. But if they do, I would say it's a bad thing to have a lot of advertisements on television, especially for sweets and sugary things.

A: I know what you mean. Children can be easily influenced to want things that are bad for them, especially if the advert has music and cartoons to amuse them as well.

B: What about giving information about products? That's quite important for consumers.

A: You're right, but do you think advertisements always tell the whole truth?

B: It depends. I suppose it's our responsibility to check out what they say.

A: That would be a problem if we had to do it for all the advertisements on television! There seem to be advert breaks every ten minutes.

B: We might be able to rely on most of them – after all, they are checked before they are broadcast.

A: True. But what annoys me is the way they interrupt a programme I'm really enjoying.

B: Yeah, I totally agree about that. There's nothing more annoying than having a dramatic moment spoiled by an advert.

A: So, maybe people who record programmes and fast forward through the adverts are being clever!

B: Yes! But the question is, are there too many advertisements on television? I'd say there are.

A: I'm not too sure about that. I think companies do need to advertise their products – that creates a good economy.

B: Hmm … You have a point, though I don't think I can agree with you.

Unit 6, Speaking Activities 1 and 2

Track 11

E = Examiner   A = Student A   B = Student B

E: I'd like you to talk about something together for about two minutes. Some people choose to do jobs that are considered to be dangerous. Here are some things they often think about and a question for you to discuss. Talk to each other about what attracts some people to do dangerous jobs.

A: OK, let's talk about this one first: high salaries. People with dangerous jobs get paid very well, don't they?

B: Yes, they do, and they deserve it. I'm not sure that the high salary is the main reason they want to do a dangerous job, though. After all, footballers get paid a lot and that's not dangerous.

A: That's a very good point – perhaps the salary isn't that important. Maybe the next one then: enjoying excitement. Some people hate routine – you know, doing the same thing every day like some people do in an office. That could be an important reason.

B: But dangerous jobs often need a lot of training, and that could be routine at first – I'm thinking that a job like a firefighter relies on everyone following the rules and they have to learn them.

A: I agree, but the job itself is not routine. When they're called out to a fire, every one is different.

B: That's true. So, you mean that 'dislike of routine' could be one of the main attractions.

A: It's possible. But how about the idea of just enjoying excitement? Some people love taking risks, and that could be a definite reason for doing jobs that are dangerous.

B: I'm with you on that – I think that excitement could be very high on the list.

A: What about needing fewer qualifications? That could be attractive to people who don't like studying.

B: I've never thought of it that way, but you may be right. And we've already said that some dangerous jobs have their own specialist training, so that could be important for some people. I don't think it's top of the list, though, to be honest.

E: Thank you. Now you have about a minute to decide which reason would make most people choose to do a dangerous job.

A: We didn't talk about doing something unusual – that could be a very good reason for someone to choose a dangerous job; they want to stand out from the crowd.

B: That's true. I think all dangerous jobs are rewarding in some way because you must feel like you've achieved something!

A: I agree with that, but I'm not sure that it's the most important reason. I'd go for excitement as the main reason.

B: I partly agree, but we also thought that dislike of routine might be important.

A: Yeah, but we thought it wasn't really crucial. We have to choose the most important reason.

B: OK. Let's stick with excitement then.

E: Thank you.

Unit 6, Listening Activity 1

Track 12

I've loved watching films for as long as I can remember, and I absolutely love thrillers and dramas. As a child, though, I used to sit on my mum's knee watching the romantic films she liked. I loved them too. My dad liked action films and when I was in my teens, I got into those too; in fact, I loved them so much I wanted to be one of the people who performed the stunts. And that's where it all began.

The profession is quite different now to how it used to be. The earliest stuntpeople weren't given any training and just had to learn through trial and error how to perform stunts. Modern action movies didn't exist at that time, so most work was in comedies – you know, like falling off a wall or something silly like that!

I didn't really think about working in the film industry until I started taking karate classes. I was doing pretty well and my teacher suggested I auditioned for a part in a movie, where the producer was looking for people with skills in martial arts to perform some stunts. I eventually persuaded my mum to let me have a go and I got the part. The rest is history.

You don't really need acting skills to do the job – which you might expect – but you do need to be very fit. Climbing or being able to ski can be really useful too – anything that will help you stand out from the crowd, really.

Working as a stuntperson is very competitive – you have to be very determined. You don't need what I call 'an action degree' or anything, but you can get into the industry by being a film extra – a kind of actor who plays very small parts in a film, like walking down a street appearing to be shopping or something. This gets you familiar with film sets and you might get to meet the stunt coordinators, who may give you work.

Being a stuntperson is hard work, and often very routine – there's a lot of waiting around. It certainly isn't glamorous, like some people think, but it's really exciting and you get to work with some great people. The best job I've done was working as a double for a famous film star who didn't want to perform her own stunts. I was fortunate to be the same height as her and with a similar figure. My hair wasn't the same though, so I had to wear a wig to look a bit more like her!

It's taken a long time for women to enter the industry, so I was really excited when I got recognised for my work. It wasn't cash or even a trophy – it was only a little statue – but it got my name known and now I'm busier than ever.

Unit 7, Speaking Activity 2

Track 13

I like these pictures! It's good to see people who are keeping fit and enjoying themselves at the same time. Both the runners and the dancers look happy. Although the people in the first picture are training hard, they are also smiling; the dancers are smiling too. But the reasons they are keeping fit in these ways are probably quite different. I mean, the runners are doing something physically hard, so you can see that they're concentrating on what they're doing. They seem to be in a park or the countryside, so they're enjoying keeping fit away from all the problems involved in running in a city. The dancers, on the other hand, are inside. Perhaps it's a dance studio and this is a regular class. It looks as though they're enjoying the movements and the music. I'm sure the dancers are happy because they're together and doing something they love as well as keeping fit. It must be very enjoyable for the people in both pictures to be able to do exercise they really enjoy, and maybe that's why they've chosen to keep fit in these ways.

Unit 7, Listening Activities 1 and 2

Track 14

1   It seems to me it isn't worth going to see the doctor these days! There are so many programmes on television about various illnesses and how to avoid getting them or what to do if you've got them. In my opinion, these programmes are really useful and I always watch them with my family and note down different things. I mean, who knows when you might catch something? The best thing is you get lots of information about unusual illnesses. There are interviews with people all over the world with health problems that you don't know anything about. It's important to be informed, don't you think?

2   I hate going to the doctor. In my experience, they don't really help you very much unless you've got something really bad and then they just send you on to see someone else! I prefer to get help from someone who knows a lot about health problems – because she's seen many of them during her life. That's my grandmother. She can always tell me what to do if I've got a cough or a headache. I like her simple, old-fashioned treatments and they usually work – much better than what people think of as up-to-date remedies. I don't think much of those!

3   When I had a pain in my hand, a friend advised me to check out a website. It was very interesting, but the best thing was all the comments people had posted about their treatments. Some of them had exactly the same problem as me. I followed the advice they gave and in two days my hand was better. My mum always goes straight to the doctor whatever's wrong with her; that's overdoing it a bit, isn't it? I mean, I know you have to be careful and that if things don't get better, it's important to go to the doctor, but this advice certainly helped me. And I didn't have to see a doctor.

4   My mother always kept a book about illnesses and treatments when I was young. It was her mother's and every time I hurt myself or had a high temperature, she would look in the book and follow the instructions. She gave it to me when I left home as a present. I must say it's very useful. It tells you when you need to see a doctor and when you can treat yourself. It's easy to understand too – without lots of difficult medical words. I know that scientists are developing more and more ways to treat illnesses but the basic problems and cures don't really change, do they?

Unit 8, Listening Activities 1 and 2

Track 15

I = Interviewer   M = Michelle

I: Michelle, you're eighteen and have a guide dog. Tell us about your dog, Rufus.

M: Yes, because I can't see very well, I have a guide dog who helps me get around – you could say he's my eyes!

I'd never had a dog before, so when I first got him, I wasn't sure how to behave around him, but he's so lovely and friendly it was easy. I wondered if he might get a bit fed up doing nothing if I was just chilling out at home, but he's really patient. I knew he'd be intelligent, though, or he wouldn't have become a guide dog. If I'm out walking and I want to go home, I just say, 'Home, Rufus!' and he takes me straight there.

I: Did you have to do any training with him?

M: Yes, I had to learn quite a few different things, like feeding him and brushing him, which wasn't too hard, but there were a lot of commands to learn – you know, like what to say to get him to do what I wanted. I kept forgetting them at first and I think he got a bit confused. I also learned how important it is to let him off the lead to go and run around for a bit and have fun – he's not allowed to do that while he's working. I was worried he might run off and never come back – but, of course, he always did.

I: What difference has having a guide dog made to your life?

M: Oh, it's completely changed my life! I can do more on my own now and don't have to rely on my parents to take me places. That means they get more free time too, so it's good for everyone. I guess the greatest change has been just not being so frightened when I'm out. I used to worry about stepping onto the road, but now I know Rufus won't let me do that. Also, lots of people stop and talk to me when I'm with Rufus, so it's nice to have that social contact.

I: How did the trainers decide that Rufus was the dog for you?

M: Well, I had a visit from the guide dog organisation and they spent some time with me, talking to me about my life and finding out a bit about my personality – things like that. I like going out and doing things, so I guess they found a dog that would enjoy that. You're also assessed to see how you walk. I don't walk very fast, so they found me a dog that would be happy at my speed. I'm quite tall as well, so it wouldn't have been much good if they'd given me a small dog!

I: And Rufus goes to college with you, doesn't he?

M: Yeah, and he loves it! He comes to most of my classes, though when I do science, he stays with a carer because he might get scared by noises or heat in the lab. My friends love him, but I do have to keep reminding them not to play with him or feed him because he might get distracted when he's supposed to be working. He can't respond to them when he's concentrating on looking after me, but I know he'd love it all if he could!

I: What do you like most about Rufus?

M: Oh, he's a great dog! I love spending time with him. When I get home from college, we mess about in the garden together. When he's off his lead, he does all kinds of silly things which make me laugh – that's my favourite thing! It's a bonus that he seems to know how I'm feeling, and he tries to comfort me if I'm in a bad mood. Luckily, my family love him too, and I feel so lucky to have him.

Unit 8, Speaking Activity 1

Track 16

Here are some things people can do to help the environment. Talk to each other about how these things can help the environment.

Now you have about a minute to decide which is the most important thing for everyone to do.

Unit 8, Speaking Activity 2

Track 17

A: So, we have to talk about how these things can protect the environment. Shall we start with 'recycling rubbish'?

B: OK. Well, obviously, recycling your rubbish is really important. It helps because then we don't put so much stuff into landfill sites.

A: What do you mean, 'landfill sites'?

B: That's what they call those great big rubbish dumps in the countryside. You know, the rubbish stays there for ages.

A: I get it. Yeah, we reuse things and don't have to use energy and new materials to make things from scratch.

B: You mean, like clothes and things?

A: Exactly. What about putting out food for birds? Do you think that's a good thing to do?

B: Sorry, I didn't catch that.

A: Do you think putting out food for birds is a good thing to do?

B: Well, yes. Because with climate change a lot of bird species are dying out.

A: Sorry, I don't follow.

B: What I mean is, sometimes the winters are harder and they can't find food; or the summers are hotter and they don't get enough water.

A: So, are you saying that it's more important to feed birds than recycle rubbish?

B: No, I'm just pointing out that a lot of our wildlife is having a bad time and it's good to help, don't you agree?

A: Um, … could you say that again?

B: It's good to help …

A: Sorry, I meant the bit about the wildlife.

Unit 9, Listening Activities 1 and 2

Track 18

Hi. I'm Ana and I want to tell you about my visit to Tech-In Expo, a virtual reality, technology and innovation exhibition I recently went to. I'd like to share my thoughts about what I saw there.

First of all, what was the exhibition? It was described in the brochures I'd read as a 'unique experience', where we could not only look at technology but also engage with it and try

things out by using virtual reality. I thought that was a bit of an overstatement – I didn't think it could be that good. I was wrong! It actually was – and it really made me think about what our lives will be like a few years from now.

The exhibition was divided into sections, or rooms, each one focusing on a particular aspect of technological progress. Some people found it frightening, others confusing but for me it was thrilling, and I couldn't wait to look at everything.

I started in the fitness room because I thought there would be loads of exciting innovations. There was a digital gym, where you could try out different exercises virtually. I had a go with a new device that monitors your performance. That sounds like existing technology that counts the number of steps you take, but the new idea is linking it to overall health. It was good, but I didn't find the device very easy to use.

Then I moved to the fashion room. I had an idea that technology was impacting the use of different materials, both man-made and natural, but I wasn't expecting to see T-shirts that actually react to your body, changing colour according to your body temperature or – even more amazingly – your mood! There were actually clothes that monitored brainwaves through tiny sensors in the fabric, changing colour according to how you felt. Amazing!

Next was the games room. Gaming isn't really my thing, but I went in because I wanted to have a go at using headsets like the ones players use in VR games. What I found very interesting was watching the technicians talking to the gamers and asking for their opinions. We're all used to giving feedback after trying a product but this was genuine conversation, to help the technicians actually build the product. It would be interesting to know how many of the gamers' suggestions will be incorporated into new games.

I was really looking forward to the robots room! Obviously, there are already factories full of robots, but I was taken with the idea of robots being able to push boundaries and do things that will be useful, not just convenient, like cleaning up the environment. I tried talking to a robot which seemed to respond to me in a natural way. That was fun at first but then it became a bit scary!

Now, the art room. I've never associated technology with art, but I found that virtual reality not only allows for technological invention and development, it provides opportunity for creativity, which I hadn't expected. In the art room there were lasers that created structures you could move through, and things hanging from the ceiling that looked a bit like ribbons. These reacted to people's movement by changing position, and to their mood by changing colour. For example, if they sensed a large group of people, they might pull back; or if a person ignored them, they might change to a really bright colour, or start flashing, to get their attention.

Another section I found interesting was the transport room. There were cars that could decide on the best route – like sat navs – but then physically direct the driver along the road. I liked that! Another thing was a series of sensors in the seatbelt that can tell whether a driver is tired or unable to drive, and stop the car moving. That pleased me because safety should always be a priority over speed or convenience.

For me, it was fascinating to see the similarities and differences between things that are now – or will soon be – part of everyday life and those we only see in science fiction. I recommend visiting the exhibition – it will really make you think!

Unit 10, Speaking Activity 2

Track 19

Discussion A

A: OK, let me think. You know, I'm not really sure. Sometimes, for me, it's better to read the book first. That's because I get my own pictures in my head about the characters. What about you?

B: Yes, I like to read the book. The reason is that a book is not only about what happens – the story or plot; it's the way it's written, how the writer makes us imagine the pictures. A film is different.

A: I agree. That's why I don't understand people who say, 'It wasn't as good as the book.' I'm not sure we should compare them because they're different.

B: Mhm. Take, for example, the *Harry Potter* books and films. They're classics now and still popular. Children still read and love the books, but they get pleasure from the films for different reasons.

A: You know, in my opinion, that's a special example. Don't you think that the books and films sort of lead into each other?

B: Yeah. That's a good point.

Discussion B

A: I feel strongly that it is very important for parents to read to their children. It helps their imaginations to grow. My mum would read to me every night and I looked forward to it a lot. How do you feel about this?

B: I couldn't agree more. It also helps the relationship between parent and child. I say that because sometimes it's the only time in the day that they have the chance to have time together. But you're right. It helps children in so many ways. For instance, my dad used to read me adventure stories like *The Time Machine* and *Treasure Hunt*, and I loved them so much I couldn't wait to learn to read myself.

Unit 10, Listening Activity 1

Track 20

N = Narrator

1

N: You hear a man and a woman talking about a play.

A: Hi there! Your new play must be starting soon. I'm definitely going to see you.

B: Well, it was the first performance yesterday.

A: Oh, that's a shame – I would have been there and wished you good luck. How did it go?

B: It was amazing! The audience loved it.

A: Well done! It's only on for a week, isn't it? I'll try to come on Thursday.

B: You'd better get your seat today though because it's really popular and I know that Friday is full already.

A: No problem. Good luck for the rest of the week!

2

N: You hear two friends talking about a television programme.

A: What did you think of the programme last night?

B: I enjoyed it. I've always liked that art style and I thought it was a great idea to go behind the scenes and show how difficult it is to organise something like that.

A: I agree. It reminded me of a film I saw once in the cinema about people who worked in a museum – it was fascinating.

B: I especially liked the pictures that one of the artists had done of that historic hotel. It would have been interesting to hear more about the history of those.

A: Exactly! Programmes like that really make you think.

3

N: You hear some travel information on the radio.

A: It's another public holiday and another busy day on the roads for drivers. Police wanted people to try to set off at different times today to avoid the big traffic jams we usually get on public holidays. Unfortunately, this hasn't happened and so we have heavy traffic on all the major routes, particularly in the south-west. An accident near the Matcham's car festival in Ferndown has closed the A31 and motorists are asked to find a different route. Traffic is also heavy in the area near Bournemouth Airport, so if you are planning to catch a flight, please allow more time for your journey.

4

N: You hear a man and a woman talking about a meal they had together.

A: I did enjoy the meal last night. Thank you very much for inviting me.

B: Thanks for coming! It is a great restaurant, isn't it? I think it's the best seafood restaurant in town.

A: You're right. My fish was grilled perfectly. But I had a bad stomach during the night.

B: I hope the fish didn't make you ill!

A: Oh no. I can't eat salmon, but I was careful to avoid that. I was just greedy and I had a big dessert as well.

B: I once had to go to hospital after eating bad fish in a restaurant. It must always be very fresh.

A: That is so true!

5

N: You hear a man leaving a voicemail message.

A: Mary? It's Charlie. I know you said you were busy tonight but we really need someone for the quiz team. David has to take his daughter to a music competition, so there are only three of us and he said I should ask you. Is there any chance you could come? Last year we won first prize when you were on the team! It would be great to do that again. It starts at seven thirty and should be over by nine. Do let me know if you can make it! I'm on 07789 785643. Thanks.

6

N: You hear a man and a woman talking about a sculpture exhibition.

A: I hear you went to the Karen Webb sculpture exhibition in Margate last week?

B: Yeah, I went with my brother just before it finished.

A: I wanted to go but I've been a bit busy recently and it's a long way, isn't it? I wish I'd gone now.

B: You'd have loved it! But you're right – it took us hours to get there and back. They had the exhibition there because Webb lived for most of her life in the town.

A: I know. I've read some books about her work. I really like her style and the materials she uses.

B: Me too.

7

N: You hear a man and a woman talking about English books.

A: My French friend wants me to recommend an English book for her to read in English. What do you think about a detective novel?

B: Yes, if she's got a good level, that would be perfect.

A: I think she's been studying English for about a year.

B: In that case, I think something like a special English book for learners might be better. You can get good, interesting stories in easy English.

A: Yeah, good idea. I was thinking about a children's book, but she might find that a bit boring. I could suggest the detective novel for later on.

8

N: You hear a man talking about buying books online.

A: I started buying books online a while ago. At first I wasn't sure if delivery would go smoothly – you know, whether things might get delayed in the post or even disappear. And people had warned me about getting the wrong books. In fact, I've found the opposite. Everything I've ordered has turned up – apart from one book that was damaged in the post and they just sent me another one free when I complained. I like buying things this way because it's quicker and easier. It doesn't cost any more than in a shop, and the payment information is always there on my computer – I can't lose it.

Unit 11, Listening Activities 1 and 2

Track 21

1 I suppose we all thought it was going to be hard, moving from a big house to a much smaller one. I used to have an enormous room at the old place and I really didn't want to have to throw away a lot of my things because they didn't fit into the new one. At first sight, it looked as if I was right, but strangely enough, the new room has been designed really well and there's actually loads of space for all my clothes and computer, TV and so on. I'd prefer to look out over the garden instead of the road, but it's nowhere near as bad as I'd thought. And it's got an amazing red carpet too.

2 We moved in a month ago but it still doesn't feel like home. It's a very modern building with three floors. My room is on the top floor and everything is new and clean and up-to-date. We've got a great security system, and the latest equipment in the kitchen. It's very high tech, which is great! I do miss the open fire in the living room we used to sit round, but I suppose I'll get used to it. At first I wasn't sure about the stone floor in the kitchen – it looks good, but I thought it might be a bit cold on the feet; actually, it's fine.

3 Our new flat in the city is brilliant! It's on the first floor and is right by a park. I spend ages just looking at the birds across there! The flat has lots of windows, so it's very light and airy. Also, there are a lot of open spaces – like, the kitchen area leads into the living area, with no walls and not many cupboards. What bothers me is not that it can get very untidy – although that is a problem sometimes – it's more that apart from my bedroom, there are no places you can just enjoy a quiet moment! I go across to the park when I want to be on my own.

4 I love the design of our new flat. It's small but it's got everything you need. It's in the middle of town, so it can be a bit noisy during the day and there aren't any trees or grass to look at! Still, I don't spend much time looking out of windows! My mum loves the wooden floors because they're easy to keep clean but I'd like to persuade her to get a carpet because, somehow, they make a room feel warmer. I know we've got good radiators but it's more about atmosphere, really.

5 I was hoping for a big room when we moved to quite a large house in the country last year and I was very happy when I saw it! It's very spacious, with big old windows and I can see right across the fields to the village. There aren't many places to put things, though, and half my clothes are in my sister's room because she's got bigger cupboards than me. It means that my room gets a bit messy with clothes over the chairs. The walls are also nice and thick and although I can sometimes hear my sister's TV, it's usually peaceful in there.

Unit 11, Speaking Activity 1

Track 22

Both pictures show people designing things, but they are completely different. The man in the first picture is designing something like a building, so I guess he's an architect. The design looks very complicated – I imagine he's concentrating very hard. The woman is also concentrating very hard, but she is obviously designing clothes, not buildings – she could be creating a new fashion! I'm sure the architect has a lot of responsibility to get things right, while the fashion designer is creating a new look that could make her a lot of money. Both of them must be enjoying their work – it's very satisfying to create something new. I guess the man gets a lot of pleasure from seeing his buildings in real life because it's very difficult work – I'd say that makes him feel very proud. And the fashion designer probably enjoys the fact that other people love wearing her clothes, and that she's making other people feel happy.

Unit 12, Listening Activities 1 and 2

Track 23

I = Interviewer   J = Jamie

I: Today on *School Matters*, I'm talking to science teacher Jamie Smith. Jamie, why did you become a science teacher?

J: I became a science teacher because I loved science lessons at school. This wasn't because I found science itself so interesting but because of my teacher. He'd start off every new topic by doing a magic trick which used scientific principles to work. He would never tell us how he did the trick, but if you paid enough attention to the experiments and things we talked about in class, you'd be able to figure it out. He made me want to be a teacher and because the things he did stuck in my head, I decided to go into science myself.

I: What do you like best about teaching science?

J: There are some useful teaching materials available and some great books that the students love. It makes teaching easier. It's that element of discovery, though, isn't it? Watching the kids work it out for themselves. I love the expression on their faces when they suddenly get an idea – you can see them thinking, 'Oh! *That's* how it works!'

I: Which science subject do you most enjoy teaching?

J: My favourite science as a kid was chemistry – I had a science kit at home and used to do experiments in the garage with my dad. That gave me a real thrill and it's something that I still love passing on to kids. Physics is inspiring – the way it helps to explain the universe – but it's based on theory and there's a lot of maths in it, which can be tricky for some, and that makes it less enjoyable to teach. Everyone loves biology because they're familiar with what's being talking about – that takes a bit of the excitement away for me, though.

I: What do you find difficult about teaching science?

J: Well, you always get those kids who just want to mess around in class – they break expensive equipment and throw chemicals around. That can be a pain. Also, the school I work in has very limited resources, so we can't buy all the best equipment, which is a shame. Most frustrating of all, though, is when I see a kid trying their best to get their head around a problem and just not getting there. That's when I get frustrated. Not at them, but for them.

I: And you're going to submit an entry to the science fair, is that right?

J: Yes! We've created an eco-car that runs on vegetable juice! I know that sounds strange but it really does work. I think we have as good a chance as anybody else to

win, but you just never know what other schools are going to come up with. I'm trying to get through to the students working on the project that they should focus on the fun they're having rather than on the possible prize at the end of it, but all they can think about is winning. I don't want them to be too disappointed if we don't.

I: Why do you think science is so important in schools?

J: Well, it explains things, doesn't it? I mean, you can actually prove stuff by demonstrating it and working things out, and that's pretty useful. Above all, there's always something different on the horizon, something new to find out. I also think it helps students to develop thinking skills and creativity, and those are things you can use in other subjects.

I: What scientific discovery would you like to have made?

J: Oh, I wish I'd discovered some kind of medicine that would cure everything. How exciting would that be? It's not because I'd have become famous or anything like that, it's just the idea of doing something that has changed people's lives for the better. I don't work in medical science, so it's unlikely I'll ever do anything like that now, but I'm definitely encouraging some of my students to go into medicine and do it for me!

Unit 12, Speaking Activity 1

Track 24

Extract A

A: How about saving money? I don't think that's particularly important, to be honest.

B: It depends on the invention. People can use inventions like computers for online shopping, which is cheaper, and that's good for everyone. And what's more, it's cheaper to …

A: I'm sorry to interrupt, but I don't think that's as important as discovering new things.

Extract B

A: How about the idea of pushing boundaries? What do you think about that?

B: I think that's a very important part of an inventor's job, don't you?

Extract C

A: … which is why I think discovering new things is vital. An inventor should …

B: Excuse me, I'd just like to say that it's important for inventors to be creative – they have to be free to try different things.

Extract D

A: If inventors create new products, they have to be made or built – and that's how new jobs are created, isn't it? And also, … Oh sorry, I didn't mean to talk for so long! Would you like to add anything?

B: Um, yes, I wanted to say that having new products to make is also interesting for the people in the workplace.

Unit 12, Speaking Activity 2

Track 25

E = Examiner   S = Student

A

E: If you could have invented something in the past, what would it be?

S1: I suppose it depends on whether I wanted to be remembered for doing something good or making money. If I wanted to do something good, then I'd choose the X-ray machine. On the other hand, the inventor who came up with hand dryers made lots of money, so I might choose that instead!

B

E: Some students prefer subjects like music or art to science. Why do you think this is?

S2: I think some students find science difficult because they have to be so accurate. It's easier to talk about a piece of music, for example, because it's just an opinion, whereas in science you have to be right. Personally, I'd love to be an inventor. It would be very exciting!

Practice Test, Listening Part 1

Track 26

N = Narrator

1

N: You hear a boy talking about a recent flight he has been on.

A: The flight itself was actually OK, in spite of all my nerves! There was quite a lot going on – you know, meals, drinks, shopping trolley – and as well as that, they had some very recent films to watch, so I didn't really notice the time pass. I thought I was going to be terrified on take-off but as it turned out, I was more excited than scared. It's such a cool experience! I hope I get to fly again sometime soon. It was a shame that we had to wait around at the airport because of the snow. Without that, it would have been a perfect journey.

2

N: You hear a woman leaving a voicemail message.

A: Hi, Jen. I know we agreed to meet up for lunch around twelve thirty, but something's come up at work and I'm not going to be able to get away for at least another hour. I've got a feeling that you need to be back at college for two o'clock, so it would make our lunch quite short! Perhaps we ought to leave it for a couple of days. What do you think? Text me when you get this message because I'll be in a meeting and I'll ring you back later. Speak soon!

3

N: You hear an actress giving an interview about a recent performance.

A: You've been getting excellent reviews for your performance in *Hamlet*, but people don't usually think of you as a Shakespearean actress.

B: True. I suppose I'm better known for my roles in soap operas on television. This was my first Shakespeare role for twenty years. I'm not sure why – I suppose it's because Shakespeare is very difficult to do well. I turned down a couple of parts a few years ago but then I was asked by Michael Barnes, a director who I very much admire, to take on this part. There was no way I could walk away from such an opportunity!

A: Well, we're all glad you didn't!

4

N: You hear a swimmer talking about a recent race.

A: It's perfectly normal to get a bit scared before a race. In fact, it's much better for your performance to have a few butterflies as it gets the adrenaline going. As a competitor, you learn to cope with that. So, that wasn't a problem for me last week. I'd done a lot of training and I was on good form, in line for the gold medal. I was standing on the blocks, ready to dive in. Then the whistle blew and off I went! It was a very good start – one of my best. But no one else was in the pool with me! It hadn't been the starter's whistle but someone in the crowd. Did I feel bad!

5

N: You hear two friends talking about the sales.

A: Did you get those jeans in the sales yesterday?

B: Yeah. I went in with Bill just before lunch yesterday, but it was a nightmare. The mall was jammed with people looking for bargains and getting frustrated because they couldn't find any. There are some good reductions but you have to look for them. I got the jeans I wanted at a great price. But when you go, avoid the main car parks because they'll be full. In fact, I'd take the bus. We had a real problem getting anywhere near the mall. And try not to get there after ten thirty. You won't be able to move!

A: Cheers. I'm having second thoughts about going at all. I may give them a miss this time.

6

N: You hear two friends talking about a recent TV programme.

A: I wasn't impressed by the first episode of the new Agatha Christie series on TV last night. I'm not sure why. It's got a fantastic cast. Did you see it?

B: Yeah. I think it's the way they've set it in the present day. For me, the story and the characters are all part of the time Christie wrote them – the thirties or forties.

A: Exactly. However well they're acted, Christie's ladies should be wearing elegant coats and smart shoes, not romping around town in jeans and boots.

B: That's it. Mind you, I'm going to watch next week's episode – I just love the guy who plays the detective. Maybe I'll get used to the setting!

7

N: You hear part of a radio news programme.

A: In spite of the weather warnings issued for the region yesterday morning, many people ignored advice to stay at home and, as a result, found themselves stranded in their cars because of dangerously icy conditions and roads blocked by minor accidents and snow. The strong winds have also brought down some power lines and at the moment, more than a thousand houses in the area are without electricity. Engineers are doing their best to restore services but it is thought that some people will have to do without power for at least another forty-eight hours. More snow and winds are forecast for tomorrow and Friday, with milder weather coming in for the weekend.

8

N: You hear two friends talking about a new laptop.

A: So, how's your new laptop?

B: I was really pleased with it when I first got it. It's so small and light I can take it anywhere – unlike my last one! Sometimes, however, it takes ages to boot up when I switch it on. Yours is the same model as mine; does yours do that, too?

A: Not now, but it was doing something similar a couple of months ago. My brother had a look at it and it's been running better since then. Shall I ask him to give you a ring? It's better than taking it back to the shop. They just send it away and you won't have it for months.

B: Great. Thanks.

Practice Test, Listening Part 2

Track 27

I'm going to tell you about my cousin's wedding in Paris. The whole family had been invited. I was excited because I'd never travelled abroad before and I was looking forward to taking the trip with my parents. My sister was disappointed not to go but she was preparing for her exams, so she had to stay at home and look after the dog.

We arrived in Paris the night before the big day. The hotel was good, though the website we'd booked it on said there was a terrace, but it was actually just a disappointing strip of pavement on the busy road. The rooms were nice, though we didn't have a good view from the window – we looked out over the dustbins at the back of the hotel!

The next day, we got up early to get ready for the day. I thought I'd packed everything I wanted to wear for the wedding – I'd coordinated everything from my hair band to my sandals, so you can imagine how irritated I was to find that I'd left my bracelet behind. It didn't really matter, but my cousin had bought it for me as a present and I wanted to wear it for the occasion.

We set off to the town hall for the wedding. I couldn't wait to see the bride and I wondered whether French weddings were similar to the ones back home. The room was full of beautiful flowers – it was the statues that drew my attention, though. They were unlike anything I'd seen before. There were some good paintings too, though not so spectacular – it was such a lovely room to get married in.

My cousin looked beautiful and the service brought a tear to my eye. Afterwards, we filed outside where the photographer took loads of pictures of the happy couple. There were loads of people around and I spotted a tourist taking photos too – it really added to the atmosphere. There was even a journalist there who knew my cousin – he was going to write an article about the wedding!

My cousin had organised a surprise for the guests before the reception. We were taken on a sightseeing tour of the city! It was good to see the monuments, though I'd seen lots of pictures of them already. What was really thrilling was looking at what everyone was wearing – Paris is known for its fashion and I'm really into it. I'd love to go back and do some shopping there.

After the tour we went to the restaurant where the reception was taking place. It had a fabulous view overlooking the river – it was so romantic. There was a band that played cool, jazz music and the tables were covered in decorations. My cousin and her new husband had done a really good job of deciding where to hold their wedding celebration.

Then we sat down for the wedding meal – I'd never eaten food quite like it. France is renowned for its cuisine and I wasn't disappointed. I'm a vegetarian and they'd made a dish especially for me. Everyone else had seafood, which I'd love to have tried, but I'm allergic to it, so I couldn't. But the dessert was amazing!

At English weddings, there are speeches. This is where people talk about the couple. It's my favourite part of a wedding, so I was a bit taken aback that it didn't happen at this one. I don't know why. They did do a first dance, though, where the couple danced to one of their favourite songs and everyone stood by, clapping and cheering.

For the rest of the evening, we danced and I had the time of my life. They played all my favourite music, including my top tune of all time, *Sunrise*. There was a DJ who you could give requests to – my dad asked for all the old stuff like *Raindrops*, and he danced around like a teenager – embarrassing! Anyway, I've brought some pictures along if anyone wants to see them.

Practice Test, Listening Part 3

Track 28

1 I'm a big fan. I've read nearly all her books once and several of them twice or more. In fact, I started reading them when I was still at high school. I remember having one open on my lap while I was supposed to be working in class! I'm not too sure exactly why I picked up the first book – it could be because I saw a friend reading one or I might have heard about them on a TV book programme, or both! All I know is that I'm hooked and I can't wait until her next one comes out. My friends are the same. But I'm the one who buys them and then passes them on!

2 It's the twists and turns in her plots that attract me to the books. They're certainly not straightforward and you can never guess the ending. I'm a bit of a crossword addict and I imagine that's why I like the books – they're real brain teasers. I don't think they come across at the cinema too well, though, although I suppose I have one of those versions to thank for getting me interested in the books in the first place! Whatever, they're definitely at the top of my list of the best books of all time. Much better than some of the books around now!

3 I can't read one of her books without being reminded of my year studying in Paris. That was when I bought my first copy of her prize-winning novel, *The Tower*. It was on our booklist for the course, but I didn't actually read it while I was in France because my French wasn't really good enough and you need to read her books in the original. So, I took it back to England with me and read it later. It definitely helped me get a better grade. I'm not sure which book is my favourite. I think it's probably that first one that I read. I'd definitely recommend her to anyone.

4 I was going on holiday last summer and I needed a good book to read on the beach, so I had a good look around the bookshop at the airport. That's when I saw her latest novel. It was quite expensive, so I hesitated between getting that one and another detective story I'd seen advertised on TV. I must admit that I chose it because it just happened to be about the same town that I was going to. I'm glad I did get it. She's a terrific writer and I can't wait to see the film when it comes out next year.

5 I had to spend some time in hospital earlier this year and I was getting totally fed up. I didn't want to do anything – read, crosswords, watch TV, nothing – especially not keep up with my schoolwork! It's difficult to get motivated about anything when you're in a hospital bed. My best mate knew how I was feeling and got me to read a novel by her favourite writer, a Swedish guy called Larsson. My favourite is usually fantasy novels and so I didn't think I'd like it much, but I loved it and couldn't put it down. Since then, I've seen the films they've made of the stories. Stunning! But not as good as the books.

Practice Test, Listening Part 4

Track 29

I = Interviewer   V = Vicky

I: Today I'm talking to Zumba instructor Vicky Baines. Vicky, what is Zumba and how did you become a teacher of it?

V: Well, Zumba's a fitness craze that's taken over the world! It's a combination of aerobics and dance done to the music of South America. I went along to a class that my friend invited me to and I was hooked. I'm sure the fact that the teacher said I was a natural had something to do with it. I had no intention of teaching it at that point, though – that was something that happened when I lost my job as a computer programmer and had to think of something else to do. I'd got tired of my boring office routine, so when I saw a course advertised, I retrained and the rest is history!

I: So, how did Zumba become so popular so quickly?

V: Well, I've got to admit that much as I love the exercise myself, the fact that it's become a craze worldwide is really unexpected. When I first started teaching, I had my doubts as to whether people would even come to the class, but I soon discovered that people are attracted to Zumba because it seems exciting. Though lots of people still prefer going to the gym or going for a run, Zumba attracts people who traditionally don't enjoy exercise.

I: Is it something that anyone can do, then?

V: Absolutely, and I've got all kinds of people in my class – from young teens to pensioners. It's a great atmosphere – the music puts everyone in a great mood and they don't even realise they're working their bodies hard. I think more than anything, people enjoy mixing with other people, much like they would at a party. Although you don't need a partner and while there are 'teach yourself' videos, it's not really something you could get much out of on your own in front of the TV.

I: How easy is it to achieve some level of success in Zumba?

V: Well, like other dances, I do think it's helpful to be able to keep time with the music, but the routines aren't based on complicated movements like more traditional dance forms are. It doesn't matter if you have limited movement either – just come along and do what you can. You'll soon loosen your body up.

I: What do you like so much about teaching Zumba?

V: The atmosphere is fantastic. I see a group of tired, ordinary people come along after work, change into their exercise clothes and come to life! I like to challenge my group by doing new combinations of the basic steps, though the moves are pretty much standard. The music is thrilling, of course – no one could resist those Latin beats – and I've bought some great compilations online.

I: What are the benefits of Zumba?

V: Zumba's a great cardio-based workout that, not surprisingly, helps to tone and sculpt the body, so it's a great way to stay in shape as well as increase strength and coordination and, believe it or not, those are things that are beneficial for day to day activities too. But it works out more than your muscles. What I didn't realise when I started out is that it has a psychological benefit too and it really does wonders for your mood. People tell other people about how they feel and then they come and join the class too!

I: So, what are your plans for the future?

V: Well, I've been asked to do a fitness video, which I actually turned down because I don't like being in front of a camera. I've just started giving classes for kids, which is exciting, though the thing I'm really becoming passionate about is something called Aqua Zumba, which is done in a swimming pool. I've got a feeling that it will become even more popular than the dance form because exercising in water works your muscles even harder.

Practice Test, Speaking Part 1

Track 30

Where are you from?

What do you like most about living there?

What sort of programmes do you enjoy watching on television? Why?

Tell me about an interesting TV programme you've seen recently.

Where is your favourite place to spend a holiday? Why?

What's the most interesting place you have visited on holiday? Why?

Practice Test, Speaking Part 2

Track 31

In this part of the test, I'm going to give each of you two photographs. I'd like you to talk about your photographs on your own for about a minute, and also to answer a question about your partner's photographs.

Candidate A, it's your turn first. Here are your photographs. They show people staying in different places on holiday. I'd like you to compare the photographs and say why you think the people might have chosen to stay in these places.

All right?

Thank you. Candidate B, which place would you choose? Why?

Thank you. Now, Candidate B, here are your photographs. They show people doing different outdoor activities. I'd like you to compare the photographs and say what you think the people are enjoying about these activities.

All right?

Thank you. Candidate A, which activity would you prefer to do? Why?

Thank you.

Practice Test, Speaking Part 3

Track 32

Now, I'd like you to talk about something together for about two minutes. Here are some ways in which people use technology today and a question for you to discuss. First you have some time to look at the task.

Now talk to each other about whether technology always makes people's lives better.

Thank you. Now you have about a minute to decide which of these aspects of technology has had the biggest positive impact on people's lives.

Thank you.

Practice Test, Speaking Part 4

Track 33

Some people say it's impossible to live without a computer today. Do you agree? Why?

Nowadays children start using mobile phones at an early age. Do you think this is a good thing? Why or why not?

Do you think technology has made people lazier? Why or why not?

Some people say that students should be allowed to use laptops in examinations. Do you think this would be a good thing? Why or why not?

Do you think technology can help us solve the world's problems? Why or why not?

Thank you. That is the end of the Speaking test.

Pearson Education Limited
KAO Two, KAO Park, Harlow,
Essex, CM17 9NA, England
and Associated Companies throughout the world

www.pearsonELT.com/gold

© Pearson Education Limited 2019

The right of Lynda Edwards and Jacky Newbrook to be identified as authors
of this Work has been asserted by them in accordance with the Copyright,
Designs and Patents Act, 1988.

New Edition first published 2019

ISBN: 978-1-292-20229-7 (Gold Pre-First New Edition Exam Maximiser)
ISBN: 978-1-292-20230-3 (Gold Pre-First New Edition Exam Maximiser
                          with Key)

Set in Frutiger Neue LT Pro Thin

Acknowledgements
We are grateful to the following for permission to reproduce
copyright material:

Text
Extract in Unit 4, page 25, from Great white shark jumps from sea into
research boat, *The Guardian*, 19/07/2011 (Rice, X.), copyright Guardian
News & Media Ltd 2018; Extract in Unit 5, page 33, from I've swapped
my paper clip for a house..., *The Telegraph*, 19/04/2006 (MacDonald, K.),
© Telegraph Media Group Limited 2006; Extract in Unit 8, page 51, from
The herd instinct, *The Guardian*, 13/06/2009 (Harrison N. and Moorhead,
J.), copyright Guardian News & Media Ltd 2018; Extract in Practice Test,
Part 6, page 86, from Faces of Everest, *The Red Bulletin*, December 2009
(Cave, A.), courtesy of Red Bull Media House.

Photos
The publisher would like to thank the following for their kind permission
to reproduce
their photographs:

123RF.com: 45, Ekachai Lohacamonchai 35, picsfive 62, toa55 37;
Alamy Stock Photo: Alex Segre 27, Bontean Magdi 19, E.Westmacott
27, Gregory King 71, Image Source Salsa 66, StockImages 9;
Shutterstock.com: Abd. Halim Hadi 40, Adam Calaitzis 69, Africa Studio
40, Anyaivanova 73, Belish 48, BonNontawat 33, CandyBox Images 95,
CatwalkPhotos 39, Daisy Daisy 74, Dima Aslanian 11, Dmitri Ma 55, Eric
Isselee 49, Happy Together 28, JGade 50, Lucky Business 95, Maksym
Povozniuk 30, RedFoxBrush 45, Robert Przybysz 46, Room27 17, Sergey
Uryadnikov 25, Slaven 70, Sofiaworld 75, Solis Images 40, Stock-Asso 45,
Syda Productions 76, TierneyMJ 54, Uber Images 44, VanderWolf Images
15, WAYHOME studio 26, anatoliy gleb 13, bokan 95, dolomite-summits
95, from my point of view 64, goodluz 13, 70, wavebreakmedia 34, 45,
wong yu liang 55

All other images © Pearson Education

Every effort has been made to trace the copyright holders and we
apologise in advance for any unintentional omissions. We would be
pleased to insert the appropriate acknowledgement in any subsequent
edition of this publication.

Illustrated by Oxford Designers and Illustrators